C000269985

To my old friend Mo
Best wishes and I
hope you enjoy

Dom B

Murder Mystery Mirth and Mayhem

Les Souvenirs de L'Inspecteur Donald Canard

and other Characters created from the imagination of

Don Balkwill

First published in Great Britain in 2020

Copyright © 2020 Don Balkwill

All rights reserved.

Interior design by Don Balkwill

Interior compiled by Sarah Elder

Cover and back designed by Les Hayes

No part of this book may be reproduced in any form or by written, electronic or mechanical means, including photocopying, recording, or by any information retrieval system without permission in writing by the author, except by reviewers who may quote brief passages in a review.

Published by Independent Publishing Network

ISBN No. 978-1-83853-596-4

Author: Don Balkwill

Email: donsphotos64@gmail.com

Address: 16 St Andrews Crescent, Abergavenny, NP7 6HL

Please direct all enquiries to the author

Printed in Great Britain

Although every precaution has been taken in the preparation of this book, the publisher and author assume no responsibility for errors or omissions. Neither is any liability assumed for damages resulting from the use of information contained herein.

Introduction

Have you ever had a scrapbook, a book where you stored your photographs and memories? Over the years I've had quite a few. The trouble is that over time they can become untidy, dog-eared, worn out, and well, scrappy; rather like me I suppose! On the other hand, a well made hardback book can last for eons. Why do I feel it is important that my memories should last for a long time? You may well ask! In a word, 'Vanity'. There are things that have happened to me in the last 25 years which I am proud of and which I hope my relatives, friends and descendants will be interested in reading about. Even if they aren't, at least I can say I put together another book and it kept me busy through the lockdown months of the Coronavirus pandemic!

There are some very special memories in the book, for example, when Marilyn and I met and eventually married, when I had a play first performed in a real theatre and when I was asked to perform the opening ceremony of a newly constructed bridge, in the area where I grew up. I'm quite proud of them all. I've never been famous and it's unlikely I ever will be, but that doesn't matter; well not that much anyway!

What promted me to put this together? Well, in November 2018, I was diagnosed with late-stage prostate cancer. After the initial furore had died down one of the thoughts that went through my head was that perhaps I should write a positive and possibly humorous account of my journey through the ups and downs of my treatment, in the hope it would help others who are going through and experiencing the same thing. In fact, a couple of people suggested it. But then I thought would anybody really want to read about what I'm going through? There's enough suffering and pain in the world, without me moaning about it. So, instead, I decided to put together a book of what I've enjoyed doing over the last 25 years. This is my scrapbook of happy memories.

Although I had done some acting in my twenties I didn't start writing or appearing in shows on a regular basis until my late 40's/50's. This came about because I had joined a social group for unattached single professionals called 'Cascade'. After a number of years in the organisation, I was approached by a chap, I think was called Carwyn (bear in mind this was 25 years ago and we weren't close friends), and asked if I had any acting experience. Carwyn wanted to put on a Murder Mystery event as entertainment for the members of Cascade. As I have always been a 'joiner-in-er', and as I had appeared in a number of amateur productions of plays and pantomimes in my early twenties, I said "yes". Unbeknown to me this was to be the start of 20+ years of murder mystery shows. We put on our first performance in November 1994 and it was a roaring success; It grew from there…..

So... this is a book of memories that are special to me, I hope you enjoy reading about them. My apologies if some of the photographs are not very clear or crisp. I've had to download many of the images from the Internet and doctor them. The originals were lost when I had a computer crash a couple of years ago. I did have backups on an external drive but that packed up too; Bit like me really!

Acknowledgments

There have been so many people who, in so many ways, have contributed to this book. Without their assistance, 'Murder Mystery, Mirth and Mayhem' would not have been possible, and so I would like to thank them all for their help.

Thanks for lending me a hand!

However, I would like to make special mention of the following:

My old friend **Les Hayes**, who not only appeared in the majority of the shows I've been involved in but also did most of the graphic design for posters, tickets, CD covers and, most importantly, designed the front and back covers of this book. I also enlisted Les's help in designing and compiling my first book back in 2006. Don't worry Les there won't be another…….. at least I don't think so!

My niece **Sarah Elder**, who had offered her help almost a year ago when I, foolishly, thought that I could do the compilation of the content myself. Sarah stepped in and sorted the problems which I was having, in what appeared to be an effortless way. I think it fair to say this book would have not been finished without Sarah's assistance.

Cenydd Hamilton, who despite his own health problems, trials and tribulations, volunteered willingly to edit and proof read the text.

Tom Gibson, who spent time and effort setting up an online platform so that I could download his photographs in the best quality possible.

Georgina Lester, who searched out photographs from fifteen years ago and made them available for the book.

Finally, **Marilyn**, my long suffering wife who not only looks after and cares for me during my illness and treatment, but has supported me unstintingly in my efforts to get the book finished. A wonderful wife! (So she keeps reminding me).

Contents

**Grapes
Of
Frath**

Back L to R: Can't remember, Graham, me.
Front: Carolyn, Can't remember, Joy, Pam, Gerwyn, Rhona

Final rehearsal before our first show

It's not that the audience
weren't paying attention,
they were trying to work out
who the murderer(s) were.

The Grapes of Frath (Nov 1994)

The first Murder Mystery in which I took part was called 'The Grapes of Frath' it was performed on 26th November 1994 in front of an audience made up of members of Cascade. You may not be aware of what Cascade was, because it is no longer in existence. Cascade was a social club for single professional people over the age of 40. The members of the group took part in various activities like guided walks, dining out and dance evenings, all with the aim of bringing like-minded people together. Well, that's what the advertising blurb said anyway! In reality, it was an organised opportunity for single mature people to meet members of the opposite sex for all sorts of social, I said social, activities, and it was very successful! But more of that later…

I was approached to take part in the show, and I agreed because I had had some acting experience in my younger days. I think the organiser, Carwyn, wrote the show and adapted the format from a boxed game.

The setting was supposed to be a luxury yacht/liner on which the suspects were travelling the world. The audience, which was sizable, was supposed to be the other passengers. The players all had crib notes from which they were to keep track of what they were meant to reveal of their part in the proceedings and any clues they might have. Everybody threw themselves into their characters, in particular the guy who was playing the ship's captain. His character was supposed to have a drinking problem and, as I was to learn later, he had clearly been type-cast. As the evening wore on, he became more and more inebriated and began to slur his words and forgot when he was supposed to reveal his clues. I was sitting next to him and found myself prompting him every time it was his turn. By the end of the evening, I seem to remember that he got the biggest applause for his convincing performance as the intoxicated Captain. Funnily enough, he never appeared in another show, not because he couldn't act but because we never saw him at a Cascade meeting ever again! My acting skills may have been too much for the gentleman to compete with!

All in all, the show was a great success and proved to be the inspiration that started me on 20+ years of writing and performing in murder mystery events, plays and pantomimes. If you would like to see this show, it is possibly still available on YouTube.'

Was Carolyn trying to influence the investigator or was she just trying to get her leg over?

A Tomb With A View

**A Comedy Thriller
by Norman Robbins**

*A once only performance before a selected audience of
miscreants, misfits and maladjusted persons dressed as their
favourite horror personality.*

Saturday 4th November 1995
St. Marys Hall, Talbot Street,
Canton, Cardiff

*Emily Tomb, a very determined lady,
played by Penny also a very determined
lady.*

*Lucien Tomb, a mad wannabee scientist
played by me with a lockdown hairstyle
before it was thought of.*

Tomb with a View (Nov 1995)

Having had so much fun with the Murder Mystery, we decided to create a theatrical group within Cascade. We gave ourselves a really original and imaginative name, 'Cascade Amateur Drama Society,' Duh! or C.A.D.S. for short, and we recruited new performers from within Cascade. We had to do this almost straight away because after just one show some of the cast had developed the 'luvvies syndrome' and threw hissy fits when their suggestions weren't followed. Strangely enough, this was mostly the men! But not my good self of course! For our next production we chose a comedy, written by Norman Robbins, and performed it on Saturday 4th November 1995 in Cardiff. The story revolved around a dysfunctional family who had a habit of murdering visitors. It all went well, apart from when the lights went out (which was intentional) and part of the scenery collapsed (which was not intentional) Marilyn Ritchie, who had just joined us said the bit she remembers most was when she had to go to check 'the fog' through a door in the wings. Unbeknown to her, as a joke, it had been 9arranged to spray dry ice straight at her. She couldn't speak for laughing! I'm still in touch with Marilyn R and a number of others from that show. Funnily enough they are all female! Unfortunately, I don't know what happened to the other photos featuring the rest of the cast. The only names I do remember of those who took part are Carolyn Gully, Rhona Hoffer, Eddie Talbot, Marilyn Ritchie, Joy Newton and Penny, who's surname escapes me. Oh! And mustn't forget Pam Allinson either, who co-directed the play with me.

Penny as Emily Tomb, Marilyn Ritchie as Anne Franklin and me as Lucian Tomb

Grapes of Frath again

Henry, Landlord of the Wheatsheaf with moustache and bowler

Above: Before the show all spick and span.
Below: Afterwards celebrating in the Wheatsheaf

Grapes of Frath again!! (Feb 1996)

Even before joining Cascade, for a number of years, I had been involved with fundraising activities at my local pub, the Wheatsheaf Inn, Llanhennock, There were some real characters amongst the regulars but nobody was more of a character than the landlord Henry. He was so laid back he was almost horizontal! Sadly he is no longer with us. Anyway, I suggested that we put on a Murder Mystery for them at the Village Hall, with the funds raised going to the nearby Cheshire Home and the local church, St John's. This was in February 1996, we used the same basic script as the one we had used for Cascade, but this show saw the birth of a character who featured in many Murder Mysteries in the future, My alter ego 'Inspector Donald Canard of the Surete'. This was just the first of many occasions when I played this character. Over the years besides being a policeman, Canard became a food critic, and then a retired sleuth who was a guest speaker at dinners and events, all so that he could be on hand to conduct the investigation and control events. He had to retire from the police forces as the years went by because you don't get many 70-year-old serving policemen do you? It turned out to be a very successful evening, with the audience really getting into character as guests on board the cruise ship. The video for this show may still be on YouTube if you are lucky.

Cast L to R. Wendy Sinnott, Colin Adams, Joan Paines, Carolyn Gully, Peter ?, Rhona Hoffer, Pam Allinson & Eddie Talbot. (Peter only did one show which is why, I expect, I've forgotten his surname).

Murder on The Mississippi

In the top picture is Joan who always supported us. The bottom right is Marilyn Ritchie who appeared in a number of CADS and CHADS shows. Still in touch.

Murder on The Mississippi (1996?)

By the time this show was performed, I had decided to play around with the Murder Mystery format as a totally separate entity from CADS. This was with the on-going aim of using it, to raise funds for good causes. It was held in the Fox and Hounds in St Mellons, Cardiff (another pub!) as an event for Cascade. I am not sure of the exact date of when it was performed, but it would have been sometime in the mid-nineties. This was an adaption of the format used in bought-in murder mystery games. Each member of the audience was given a name as they came in and they were also given envelopes, which contained clues, to open throughout the evening. Nobody, not even the murderer, knew who the guilty party was until the end of the evening. As the setting was a riverboat on the Mississippi the audience came dressed in Wild West costumes which added to the fun. Even though it was quite complicated and a little convoluted the participants enjoyed themselves. However, I decided I would simplify the format in future productions.

The saloon girls showing a bit of leg. Raydene Blackmore on the right appeared in a number of shows, we are still in touch.

Vanessa on the left and friend. If you've got it flaunt it, and why not?

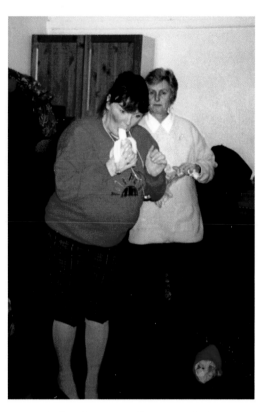

Eddie as Snow White, Marilyn R as the Footman & Gwyn as Excretia, the Witch, it's a devil of a job to get a bra that fits.

Liz Gallagher teaching Judy how to get a whole banana into your mouth without choking, or is she?

The undertakers collect the poisoned Snow White. The shorter of the two was played by Joan Paines who is an undertaker in real life, typecast or what?

Snow White and the Seven Dwarfs the Adult Version (Nov 1996)

This was our first attempt at writing a Pantomime for adults, I won't bore you by explaining the plot because you all know the story of Snow White, we just made it more adult orientated. Pam Allinson, Liz Gallagher and I spent many evenings laughing our socks off whilst we were writing this production. The show was performed for two nights in November 1996 and the proceeds went to Children in Need. We had a 6ft 3 ins male, Eddie Talbot, playing Snow White and all the dwarves were females under 5 ft 2in. The highlight of the show was the scene where the wicked witch, superbly played by Gwyn Jenkins, tries to poison Snow White, but, instead of a poisoned apple, our version had a poisoned banana! The witch tries to tempt our heroine into taking a bite from the banana (use your imagination), it was hilarious. If you want to have a look at the video it may still be on YouTube. As you can see from the photographs, we had a lot of fun performing this show, the audience laughed a lot, we laughed a lot, and the after show party was terrific. What makes this show a truly notable event as far as I'm concerned is that I met my wife to be, as a result of it. I was at a Cascade meeting and was looking for people to appear in the show, in particular I was looking for women to play the dwarves. I was introduced to a young lady by the name of Marilyn and I tried my best to recruit her. It's fair to say I piqued her interest and she agreed to join us but she didn't appear as a dwarf, she had a special role playing the piano dressed as a French maid. Oh, La La! From now on I shall call this lady Marilyn L, so she won't be confused with the other Marilyn, Marilyn R. I can't remember how much we raised for Children in Need but I do know it was a goodly sum.

Six of the seven dwarfs, Judy, Raydene,Wendy, ?,Joan and Rhona. Martin as Goldilocks, Marilyn R as the Footman and me as the Fairy. The other dwarf was Liz who was busy with a banana see facing page.

I'm sorry about the quality of the photographs but bear in mind that these were taken in the early days of digital photography.

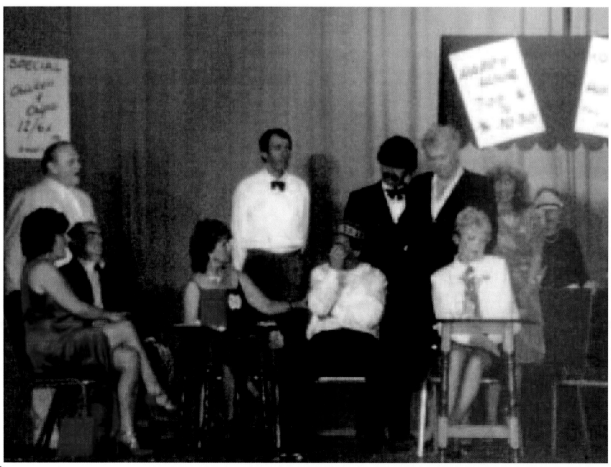

The Mates Murder (June 1997)

The first Murder Mystery I wrote on my own, was actually a stage play. It was performed exclusively for members of Cascade, this was in June 1997. Surprise, surprise, the setting for the play was a singles club disco dance, They do say you should always write about something you know about. (Just a thought, who are they?). It had all the ingredients of the Murder Mysteries we were to perform in later years - all the characters had motives to commit the murder and they all try to implicate each other. The main difference was that I wrote all of the dialogue. In later murder mysteries the actors were just given details of their background, their dark secrets and the details of their accusations. All the other dialogue was ad-lib. In this show I played the ghost of the murder victim so that I could be on stage most of the time to act as prompt when the 'actors' forgot their lines, which, as you can imagine, they frequently did. Well, we were very much amateur players. Marilyn R, who played the detective says she remembers this show well because during the interval a man told her, rather seriously, that no way could the victim have screamed if she had been poisoned with that particular substance. Which is all very strange when you consider that the murder victim was male (me) and had been stabbed! Marilyn did try to explain to him he had got it wrong and it was all just for fun anyway, but he was having none of it.

I'm sorry but as with a lot of other shows I can't remember the names of most of the characters (and some cases the actors), but here goes from L to R the actors:
Joan Paines, John Owen, Me (standing), Rhona Hoffer, Ian Phillips (standing), Gwyn Jenkins, Colin Adams (standing), Forgotten name, Wendy Sinnot, Judy ? (at rear), and far right sitting Raydene Blackmore.

Cinderella, (Wendy Sinnott) disappoints poor old Buttons again, (John Owen).

Typical woman once she has had a Prince nothing else will do!

Family love in. Sandy played by me, Nastasia played by Joan and Francis played by Eddie.

The King (Ian) always liked to get to grips with the French maid (Marilyn)

The C.A.D.S. present
A CHARITY PERFORMANCE
The Adult version of

CINDERELLA

An everyday story of the escape from bondage of a beautiful maiden with rampant hormones, who is held in the evil clatches of her bent brothers and depraved step-mother
on
Friday 9th January 1998
St. Mary's Hall, Talbot St, Canton, Cardiff

Performance starts 7.30pm   Tickets £4.50

Tickets only £4.50 what a bargain for an evenings entertainment

12

Cinderella, the sequel (Jan 1998)

Our next show was another pantomime performed in January 1998, 'Cinderella, the Sequel' written by Pam Allison and myself. Our thinking was, what actually happened after Cinderella found her Prince, did they live happily ever after as in most modern fairy tales? Or was there a darker element as in the tales of old? Well not to keep you in too much suspense, in our version, no, they didn't end up happy ever after. They had split up and Cinderella went back to live with her evil stepmother. Instead of stepsisters, she had proudly gay stepbrothers. Eddie Talbot and I played the brothers, Francis and Sandy, and we really camped it up, which Marilyn L, my girlfriend by now (I am sure you saw that coming), found very disconcerting. In our show, we had characters from various other pantomimes visit as well as a singer who couldn't sing. She brought the house down. We even had not one, but, wait for it, two Fairy Godmothers, "Oh no you didn't". I can hear you all say, "Oh yes we did", and we named them, Fairy Snow and Fairy Liquid. They were played with much gusto by Marilyn R and Anne-Marie Winslade. Once again it may be still available on YouTube.

Eddie, Wendy, Jackie, Rhona and Joan backstage with Mother Theresa! (Look at the wall)

One of the many highlights of this pantomime was Pauline Beer who played the singer, Donna Louise El Marco del Monte. Throughout the show one character or another would use a line from a well known song and then say "You know they ought to write a song about that" and then Pauline would rush on and say "They did" and burst out with a verse or two of the song. Only trouble was she couldn't sing! It was hilarious she brought the house down every time she came on.

Ian Phillips, a schoolteacher, playing a schoolteachers checking his notes

Above, Jonny Smith, as Joe, apparently didn't need to use notes!
Below, Elaine Evans, amother teacher, played the gym mistress.

Larnings School (Oct 1998)

Due to the success of the 'Grapes of Frath' performed for Llanhennock in 1996, I was asked to put on another murder mystery in 1998 to raise funds; this time for Llanhennock Village Hall. I can't remember why, but the format for this one was as follows: The setting was, as the name suggests, at a school called Larnings (A good start I hear you say), where the Headmaster gets murdered. Members of the staff, including the kitchen staff, all of whom had motives to commit a murder, are present. The youngest suspect was Joe Felloni played by 16-year-old Jon Smith, my stepson to be, he did an excellent job, if I say so myself, with no bias or £20 bribe from the wife.

After the introduction of the characters, who were also the suspects, each moved around from table to table, so the audience could question them individually. The investigation was coordinated once again by Inspector Canard. Marilyn L who played the matron of the school said one of the most disconcerting and possibly funniest moments for her was when she sat at a table where two young children no more than 11 years old were sitting. Without batting an eyelid they grilled Marilyn like two seasoned professionals, suggesting that she had an affair with the murdered Headmaster! What I want to know is what do children of that age know about affairs for goodness sake?

Marilyn Lewis, as she was then, another school teacher in her first murder mystery, played the school matron. It's amazing the number of teachers involved in amateur dramatics, is it because they want to be somebody else?

Wendy on the left, unknown skeleton dancers, and John Owen on the right.

Above: the Finale
Below: Marilyn helps Wendy fix her earrings whilst Joan grows her mustache

Aladdin (Jan 1999)

In January 1999 we performed what was to be our third and final pantomime for Cascade. "Oh no" I hear you cry, "Oh! Yes, it was!" This was adapted by other members of the CADS team who felt they would like to have a go at writing and producing a show. We were getting quite ambitious by now and we even hired in the appropriate costumes for this Arabian themed show. Marilyn L played Princess Janine opposite Jackie Dafon who took the male lead of Aladdin. I played Widow Twankey and had to wear a dress and a blonde wig again. I think it was the loss of my own hair that had created in me the desire to wear a wig, the dress was just a bonus!

Ian Phillips, who played the baddy Abanazar, recalls he was playing his guitar and a drudge of skeletons (I didn't know that 'drudge' was the collective term for skeletons did you? I would have thought that a 'rattle' sounds much more apt), came on too early so he had to improvise and send them off before resuming his song. Well, we were all amateurs. Once again you may find the video on YouTube. The proceeds of this show were donated to Kidney Research UK.

Me as the Widow, Martin as the Genie, and Pauline as the slave of the ring.

Rhona as Hoo Sit, Jackie as Aladdin, and Wendy as Abdul.

Joan as Mustapha, Wendy as Abdul, and Ian as Abaanazer.

Rhona as Hoo Sit, Jackie as Aladdin, and me as Widow Twankey.

17

Harvest Festival Auction Produce

The donated produce was a mixture of home grown fruits, vegetables, plants etc, and shop bought items.

The highlight of the auction was the selling off, of the harvest festival loaf in the shape of a sheaf of corn which was always made in the local bakery in Caerleon. It can't really be seen from the photograph but there was the shape of a little mouse on the sheaf. The produce was sold off first using the traditional type of auction method where the highest bidder wins and pays the amount bid.

However, as the final lot of the day we sold off the harvest loaf using a single bid style of auction. This is how the auction worked. There would be four or five people situated throughout the pub with buckets. The bidding was in pound coins only. If you wanted to bid, you had to throw a pound into the bucket. The auction was supposed to be timed, and whoever threw the last pound into the bucket when the time was up won the harvest loaf. The truth of the matter is that I kept the auction going until I felt that I had milked all I could from the audience. On a number of occasions over £200 was raised for this part of the auction alone. Not a bad return for a loaf of bread!

Harvest Festival Auctions, Llanhennock (1992-1999)

I had been visiting the Wheatsheaf Inn, in Llanhennock, since the late eighties, purely for the ambience of course, and as mentioned previously I had become involved in their fundraising activities almost immediately. One of the highlights of their year was helping with the Summer Fayre held by the Leonard Cheshire home, which was located just down the road from the pub. As you may be aware, this charity supports disabled people through local care services, including residential homes and numerous other services. You should go and discover the remarkable story of Leonard Cheshire who was a World War II fighter pilot with the RAF and suffered serious injuries during the conflict. As part of the summer fayre activities the owners of The Wheatsheaf, Marge and Henry, would hold a Harvest Festival auction, where locals donated produce, with the proceeds of the auction going to the Cheshire Home. Year after year there were a number of regulars who always took part and gave very generously. In the early nineties, besides being involved with the Summer Fayre selling raffle tickets, I was roped into becoming the auctioneer for the donated produce. I carried out this task for several years until I moved out of the area when Marilyn and I set up home in Abergavenny.

As you can see, just about, from the photograph I was balanced precariously on a wooden stool, something I could never do today, Oh! To be young again.

The Charities Amateur Dramatic Society
present

THE WATERSHED

A musical comedy by local writers Don Balkwill and Jane Laurenti

The plot revolves around the hilarious and bizarre efforts of a group of geriatrics to murder the prospective owner of their retirement home, "The Watershed"

Friday 7th September 2001

At The Borough Theatre, Cross Street, Abergavenny

Performance begins at 8.00pm.

Ticket £5.00, available from the Box Office, Abergavenny 01873 850805

ALL PROCEEDS IN AID OF THE LEUKAEMIA RESEARCH APPEAL FOR WALES

If you are connected to a registered charity and would like to raise some funds by having a free performance of this play contact Don Balkwill Tel: 01873 859017

Jane as the Matron, Hilda Coldtitz, after she crashed her car. The residents had tampered with the brakes thinking that the car belonged to Rupert DeBear.

Marilyn R as Mrs Wrinkleworth, Jane, as Matron, Jackie as Nurse Lovechild, Marilyn L. as Dilys Pandy, Joan as Miss Witless and Martin as Hurley.

20

The Watershed (2001)

Sometime during the year 2000, Marilyn and I were having a fish and chip supper in a small restaurant in Usk. In one corner was another couple and they appeared to be having a domestic argument. I glanced over and the lady caught my eye, I smiled and made some comment about relationships. The lady, who we later learnt was called Jane Laurenti, replied that they weren't a couple and that they were just friends having a disagreement. Anyway, we got talking and the upshot was that we introduced Jane, who was also single, to Cascade and roped her into our theatrical group. Jane and I then wrote a play together called 'The Watershed'. The story revolved around a group of pensioners who live in the Watershed, a retirement home for single people. The owner of the home, Ted DeBear, has been missing for seven years and is about to be declared dead. His nephew, Rupert DeBear, will inherit the home and his plan is to sell it off so it can be redeveloped as a supermarket. On learning of this, the residents make a number of inept attempts to kill off Rupert. Everyday 'goings-on' at most nursing homes I guess! Luckily, a missing will is found before Rupert DeBear can succeed, and one of the staff at the home inherits everything instead and everybody lives happily ever after, or do they?

We performed the Watershed at five different venues in 2001, raising funds for six different organisations including, Llanhennock Cheshire Home, Craig Community Hall, Leukemia Research Appeal for Wales, Caring for Carers, NSPCC Wales, and Hearing Concern. The only photographs I have of this time were taken during rehearsals for the show in Llanhennock Village Hall. Incidentally, during this time we had renamed ourselves CHADS, The Charities Amateur Dramatics Group because so many of our group had left Cascade.

Background: Two Marilyn's & Gwyn Jenkins (seated) as Rupert DeBear.
Jane and I in the foreground discuss the show.

Launch of the Pantomonium website (April 2001)

At the time in 2001, one of the things I found frustrating was the thought that the plays, pantomimes and murder mysteries that we were writing were in the most part being performed once and then the scripts were cast aside. My thought was that there must be other people around the world like ourselves, who just wanted to enjoy themselves by performing and at the same time raising some funds for good causes. There are businesses that supply scripts for amateur use, but these have to be paid for. Also there are the royalties that have to be paid for putting the show on. So the idea of making our scripts available free of charge to whoever wanted them came about. The story of how this happened in 2001 is in the newspaper story below. All I asked for in return was that the recipients let me know if they had used a script and that we were acknowledged as contributors. I also asked that, if possible, they provided a video of the show. In the following two years, having sent out dozens of copies of scripts, I received only a few acknowledgments and three videos, two from Australia and one from America. It was very frustrating, particularly the American one. They had adapted the script (The Watershed) which was fine, but in the credits, our input was not acknowledged at all, and the producer claimed to have written the play herself! I, therefore, decided to close down the website as it had not lived up to my expectations for it. You may wonder what happened to all the scripts that we wrote. Well, sorry to say they were all lost when I had a computer crash. "Didn't you do backups?" I hear you cry. Yes I did, they were all copied onto a remote USB hard drive, but guess what, that packed up too!

Don's scripts for charity fund-raising shows now going world wide

AN amateur playwright who lives in Abergavenny, is finding that scripts he wrote and co-wrote for charity fund-raising shows are in demand by other fund-raising groups throughout the English speaking world via the Internet.

Don Balkwill who lives at Coldbrook, has been writing scripts and producing plays, pantomimes and murder mysteries to raise funds for charities and good causes for the last six years.

Rather than see the scripts, once performed, never used again, he decided to set up and Internet site to make the scripts available free of charge to other amateur groups to use as fund raisers. He set up his first site in February 2000, not only to make his scripts available, but also to encourage other amateur playwrights to make script available through his site.

After a slow start, there has been a sudden burst of interest in the website

since he decided to revamp it earlier this year. He had some new play scripts to add and being very much an amateur in website design, he rang a friend for advice.

His friend in turn passed him on to one of his friends. "When I phoned this friend, a Nic Carter-Jones, I was unaware who he was," explained Don.

"I asked Nic which design package he would recommend and he asked me what I was trying to achieve. I explained that I raised money for charity by putting on pantomimes and plays and what the purpose of the Internet site was.

"Nic offered to redesign the web site, give it a new name and simpler address,

host it, maintain the site and incredibly waive all his normal fees. As you can imagine I was astounded," said Don.

"It turns out that Nic is the owner of New Millennium Internet Services Ltd, a web design and hosting service based near Brecon."

Since the new site, WWW.Pantomonium.co.uk has been active, enquiries and submissions have increases significantly," said Don. "I have already supplied scripts to groups in North America, Canada, Australia, Israel and Eire, besides requests from all over the UK," he said.

"I'm hoping that as the site becomes better known, more and more playwrights will contribute. It

all links in with by being the producer for CHADS - Charities Amateur Dramatic Society - because 'it would be useful to have a choice of new shows available for next year.

"We are currently performing one of our melodramas, 'The Watershed' which is set in a retirement home and revolves around the hilarious and inept attempts of the residents to murder the prospective new owner of the home," said Don.

"We have already performed it and raised £430 for the Llanhennock Cheshire Home. We shall be performing the play at various venues in South Wales to raised funds for the NSPCC, Cancer Research Wales, Hearing Concern and the Thb Graig Hall, Bassaleg."

If there are any other good causes that want to raise funds, or if any person is interested in getting involved with CHADS, they should contact Don through the Internet site, or by telephone on 01873 859017.

•Don is pictured at his computer with his new Internet site on screen.

No Sex Please, We're British (June 2002)

In December 1999, I came to live in Abergavenny and, about a year later, joined Abergavenny Theatre Group after being invited to one of their social evenings by Jane Laurenti, who was already a member. I enjoyed the evening so much, I decided to join them and soon became heavily involved. The following year I became a committee member, and then became Chairman a year after that. My first acting role for the group was as a Police Inspector in 'No Sex Please, We're British' playing the part of Superintendent Vernon Paul, in the Spring 2002 production. It was performed in Abergavenny Borough Theatre, the towns main performance venue. The Beatles even appeared on stage there back in the nineteen sixties.

I roped Marilyn into the show as the 'Customer service agent' a joyful euphemism for a 'lady of the night', which in itself is another euphemism! Thinking about it I've played policemen in most of the productions I've appeared in. Do you think this is because I always want to be in a position of authority and order people around? Surely not!

Back: Tony Tagg, Janet Richards, Marilyn L. and me
Front: Rob Tollman and sorry I've forgotten her name.

Murder at Llanwenarth Hall (January 2003)

During the early 2000s I hadn't written or taken part in any murder mysteries because I was quite heavily involved with Abergavenny Theatre Group. One of my main tasks was fund-raising for them, because although some productions made a small profit, most only broke even and some even lost money. So, in 2002 I suggested, that I write a murder mystery which could be used as a fund-raiser for the group. This was agreed. The setting for the murder mystery was the 1946 AGM of a fictitious theatre group called the Sugarloafers. The plot revolved around the petty jealousies, back-biting, and the intrigues you can get in theatrical groups. (Where I got the ideas for this, I couldn't possibly say). The show was performed on 25th January 2003 in Llanwenarth Hall. The audience was made up of members of ATG and their friends. It was a roaring success. Unfortunately, as far as I'm aware, there were no photographs taken. All I have are parts of the programme. I played the investigator 'Richard (Don't call me Dick) Head', another character that appears quite frequently in future murder mysteries.

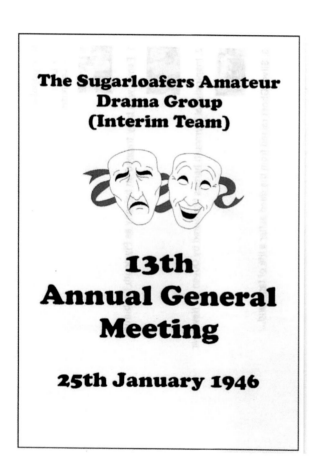

The Sugarloafers Amateur Drama Group (Interim Team)

13th Annual General Meeting

25th January 1946

Your Committee

Chairperson	**Roberta Henshaw.** Founder member of SADGIT Takes a leading role. Formerly a professional actress.
Treasurer	**Vernon Crook.** A long standing member Keen actor. Has appeared in most of our productions.
Secretary	**Vanessa Shaw.** A talented young actress who only joined us 18 months ago. Stepped in as Secretary at short notice.
Committee	**Miles Haway.** Director of our last 2 productions, Formerly worked professionally as a Director and Actor. Joined us only a year ago.
	Fiona Frockhart. Another founder member with no desire to act, but enjoys being the Wardrobe Mistress.
	Carl Poynter. Long standing member of the group. Both actor and sometimes Director.
	Amanda Starr. One of our newest members, very keen, very enthusiastic, with aspirations to be a pro ffessional actress.
Our Guests	**Richard Head.** Chief Constable for the area.
	Ruby Hareng. Theatre critic and reporter

I thought the name of the group, 'Sugarloafers Amateur Drama Group Interim Team' was particularly appropriate when turned into an acronym. (Think about it).

Murder at the NSPCC (Nov 2003)

Back in 2001, CHADS had performed 'The Watershed' in Ponthir Village Hall to raise funds for the Ponthir branch of the NSPCC. That performance raised £581.00, which was the most amount of money that the branch had ever raised from a single event. As a result, I was asked, if I would put on another show, so I suggested we did a Murder Mystery rather than a play. The setting for this one was at a committee meeting of the NSPCC, where the Chairperson is murdered. Regrettably, there are no photographs for the performance, which took place in November 2003, but as you can see from the letter below it was a great success, and set a new record for funds raised from a single event. Incidentally, the addresses have been removed purposely which is why certain areas appear smudged.

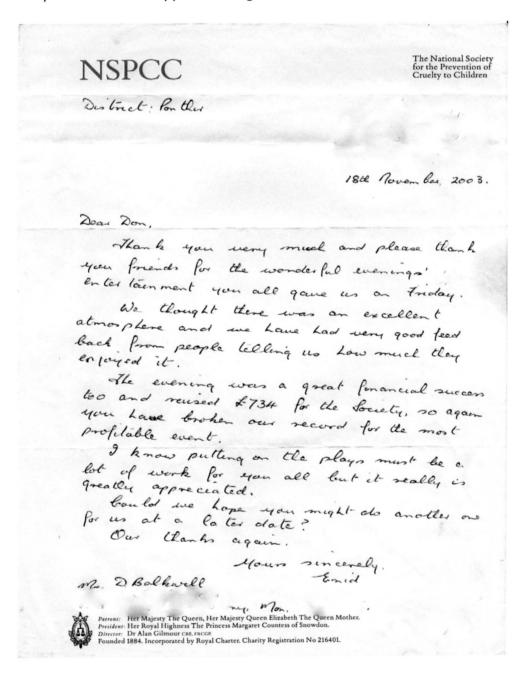

The cast with members of Soroptomists and volunteers from Glamorgan Railway Company

Soroptimists International, Barry & District present

Murder on the Island Express

The Characters

Major Richard Smythe. (The Victim) Mid 50's. Distinguished war record. Served with SOE behind enemy lines. Married with 1 son. Was manager of the local Bank but retained title of Major in preference to Mr. Married to Olivia and father to Richard. Considered himself to be a bit of a ladies' man.
Played by John Morris

Olivia Smythe. Mid 50's Wife of Major Smythe and mother of Richard (Little Dickie). Left a substantial estate by her late father. Does not work but considers herself to be a pillar of the community. President of the Soroptimist's. Invited Inspector Canard on the outing because he was visiting her husband.
Played by Rhona Hoffer

Richard (Dickie) Smythe. Aged 23. Son of Major and Mrs Smythe. As an only child he was very spoilt. University educated. He is currently between positions. Volunteered to help his mother with the organising of the day out.
Played by Matt Beere

Vernon Marks. Late 40's Assistant Bank Manager to Major Smith. Ex-army. Married to Olwen but no children. Supportive of Olwen whenever there is a Soroptimist function that requires an extra hand.
Played by Gwynn Jenkins

Olwen Marks. (Nee Lewis). Mid 40's Married to Vernon but previously married to one of his friends who died in the war. Has 2 businesses, a hairdressing salon and a local café. Treasurer for the Soroptimists.
Played by Marilyn Lewis

Mary O'Connell. Late 40's. A widow whose husband died in the war. Has a small accountancy practice that she runs from home. Recently returned to the area with her sister Lydia to nurse their ailing parents. Has a daughter Jenny. Secretary for the Soroptimist's.
Played by Pamela Allinson

Lydia Osbourne Late 40's Also a widow who's husband died in the war. Works in a solicitor's office. Recently returned to the area with her sister Mary to nurse their ailing parents. Member of Soroptimist's. Mother of Joan.
Played by Carolyn Gully

Jenny O'Connell Mid 20's. Daughter of Mary, very close to her. Unmarried schoolteacher. Came to the area with her mother. Helps out with Soroptimist functions. Her best friend is her cousin Currently has no boyfriend.
Played by Jodie Allinson

Joan Osbourne. Mid 20's Daughter of Lydia. Works in local bank for Major Smythe. Also came to the area with her mother. Very close to cousin Jenny. Unmarried but has a boyfriend who works in bank HQ.
Played by Emily Underwood

Inspector Donald Canard of the Surete. Mid 50's Visiting his old friend Major Smythe whom he served with in the SOE during the war.
Played by Don Balkwill

Devised and Produced by Don Balkwill, "Made to Measure Murders"
Telephone Abergavenny 01873 859017

Program and ticket

Murder on the Island Express (July 2003)

Pam Allinson, with whom I had written the pantomimes, was a member of Barry Soroptomists, a worldwide volunteer service organization for women who work for peace, and to improve, the lives of women and girls, in local communities. Pam asked if we would be prepared to put on a Murder Mystery event to help them raise funds for Cancer Research UK Cymru. We of course agreed. Pam suggested that we set the murder mystery on board the Barry Island Steam Train, which was run by volunteers. I duly wrote the Murder Mystery with a plot that revolved around a Soroptomists annual outing set in 1955. The Chairperson's husband, Major Smyth, is found stabbed to death in the guards-van of the train. The investigation was carried out by none other than Inspector Donald Canard of the Surete in the station waiting room. Incidentally, the train journey was only four minutes long because of the length of the track available, so we did the journey twice! The victim was played by John Morris. Poor John had to be stabbed twice, Perhaps I should have called it 'You Only Die Twice' - maybe it could have been turned into a film? The person missing from the cast photograph is Gwyn Jenkins who played the part of Vernon Marks. This was because he was late turning up. We were having kittens wondering if he would ever arrive! He did, just before the train pulled out of the station!

All the cast members for this production were either Ex-Cascaders or their friends, and it was performed on 11th July 2003. The show steamed along and everybody was really chuff, chuff chuffed. Also, by this time CHADS had been disbanded because we all lived so far apart and were involved in other things. I was also looking for a name for a murder mystery group and I came up with 'Made to Measure Murders' as an interim choice. Obviously I didn't think much of it because I never used it again.

Rehearsal L to R. John Morris as Major Smyth, Marilyn L as Olivia Marks, me as Inspector Canard and Gwyn Jenkins with back to us as Vernon Marks.

The Golden Gun Awards for 1920

*Llanhennock Hall, a traditional village hall, it looks like a room
full of suspects rather than an audience*

*Emma-Jayne as the victims daughter, Tony as his brother, Marilyn as brother's
Fiancee, Oliver as the son, Carolyn as the grieving widow, Me, at the back as the
Godfather. Missing is John who has nipped out for more wine or was it a pee?*

The Golden Gun Awards for 1920 (Feb 2004)

Following the success of 'Murder at Llanwenarth Hall' the previous year, I was asked to put on another Murder Mystery for the theatre group on Valentine's day 2004. This time the setting was an Italian restaurant owned by a Mafia hitman in the 1920s in the USA. The theme was a sort of gangster version of the Golden Globe Awards, which was renamed 'The Golden Gun Awards for Hitman of the Year 1920'. (What a mouthful). In my version, the hitman didn't get his award because he got bumped off. Tony Tagg and John Geraghty made their debuts in this production; the first of many appearances in our murder mysteries. A very talented (and young) Emma-Jayne Morris (nee Williams) played the daughter but didn't appear in another murder mystery until eleven years later. Oliver Haswell played her brother, and he so enjoyed it that he wrote a murder mystery, which ATG performed a year or so later. Sadly, because of work commitments, Oliver never appeared in another of my murder mystery shows. Carolyn Gully from CHADS came all the way from Barry to play the part of Mama, and Marilyn L. played the part of Olivia. I played the Mafia Godfather Don Cortesone, who carried out the investigation. What made this show particularly funny was that when the audience wanted to ask a question they had to do so with an American, Italian or Irish accent. Another hit (pun intended)! This was the first of many performances of this particularly popular Murder Mystery. Unfortunately, the photographs are all very similar and were taken from the back of the hall, I've tried my best to enhance them.

This gangster gaff served some good Italian wines, which the cast insisted on sampling.
Emma-Jayne Morris, Tony Tagg, Marilyn Balkwill, Oliver Haswell, Carolyn Gulley and
John Geraghty decide to test them..

Granddaughters Josie, Kirsty and Gemma chase bubbles whilst the new Mrs Balkwill and my son Mark, looks on.

The traditional group photograph taken in Abergavenny Castle.

Our Wedding (July 2004)

You may wonder what photographs of our wedding are doing in a scrapbook of Murder mysteries, plays, and books. Well, I did say in my introduction that this book contains some very special memories for me, and our wedding is one of those times, and, as this is my book I wanted to include it. So there, (stamps foot). It was a wonderful two-day event held in July of 2004. Firstly, the wedding ceremony was performed in the Angel Hotel. This was followed by photographs in the ruins of Abergavenny Castle. Then back to the hotel for the reception and evening party. The following day we had a picnic during the day in the grounds of the Castle, with an evening party for more friends at the 'King of Prussia'. We had glorious weather throughout. A joyous and memorable two days and we have remained happily married to this day (well most of the time, so my wife tells me).

We have been married for 16 years last July and at the time of writing we had just finished twelve weeks of lockdown and we are still talking...... and laughing.

LIES SEX & DISCOTHEQUES
a 'who dunnit' comedy of bad manners
BY DON BALKWILL

Running time 62 minutes

It's just after midnight in the Seabonk Hotel and the members of "Mates", the seaside town's premier singles club are dancing the the night away at their monthly hormone packed Disco. Meanwhile Ed Armbuster, the clubs organiser, has checked out somewhat prematurely and permanently. Inspector Clewes interrogates the suspects in the Hotel's Lounge... but why not the beautiful leather-clad woman seated in the corner?

Cast in order of appearance

Crusty Pratt: Announcer	TONY MONAGHAN
Cindy Cravesit	KIRSTY FLYNN
Bonnie Butt	LOUISA CONNELLY
John Crapper	ALAN WILSON
Richard Dixon	LES HAYES
Ivor Bordello	TONY TAGG
Inspector Clewes	JOHN GERAGHTY
Judy Watchors	JANET RICHARDS
Sherry Tippler	LYNN JONES
Ed Armbuster	NICK WATKINS
Sara York	SAMANTHA CHRISTIAN
Phil McCaffity	CHRIS GRAY
Liza Lott	EMMA WILLIAMS
Eva D'eath	HELEN GERAGHTY

Lies, Sex & Discotheques was written, adapted for radio and directed by Don Balkwill and was recorded at the Borough Theatre Abergavenny on Saturday 22nd January 2005.

Grateful thanks to Stage and Technical Manager, Ioan Wynne, who was responsible for sound recording and effects.

Our thanks also go to Nick Banwell, Manager of the Borough Theatre, to the Theatre Management Committee and to Monmouth County Council for their support for this project.

All proceeds from sales of this CD are used to support future productions.

Graphics by Les Hayes at Hannibal Graphics t: 01291 690901 e: les_hayes@mac.com

Copyright of this production remains entirely with the author. The work may not be reproduced or broadcast in any other form or media without the express permission of the author.

It didn't matter that there was scenery in the background, we were recording a CD.

CD Recording of Lies, Sex and Discotheques (Jan 2005)

In 2004 I put forward my play 'The Mates Murder' to be performed by ATG as their Autumn production. At that time the 'old guard' on the selection committee didn't believe in using plays written by unknown playwrights, so another play was chosen instead. The fact that it was 'Tartuffe', one of the most famous theatrical comedies by Molière had nothing to do with it! But, whilst discussing my offering somebody suggested, because of the amount of dialogue, and because there was so little physical action in it, that it would make a good radio play. From that developed the idea of recording a CD of the play and selling copies of it to raise funds for the theatre group. I approached the manager of Abergavenny Borough Theatre, Nick Banwell, and explained the concept, that we needed the use of a stage and some recording equipment, but didn't have a lot of funds to spare. Nick was very sympathetic. He offered us the use of the theatre on a Saturday morning, provided, we could get the permission of the Theatre Management Committee and Monmouth County Council who owned the theatre. This we duly did. In the meantime, I rewrote the script to take account that the listener couldn't see any set or the performers. So I introduced an announcer to set the scene. I also felt that the show could do with a different title and asked around for ideas. It was Les Hayes who came up with 'Lies, Sex & Discotheques'. He also designed the covers and CD label and appeared in the show. All of which, I thought was brilliant. The play was duly performed and recorded on Saturday 22nd January 2005. Everybody who took part thoroughly enjoyed themselves and copies of the CD were made and sold for the princely sum of £4.95 each. They were also on sale at future ATG performances. I am sorry to say there are now no more copies available, even if you wanted one. However, I hope there will be a copy available on YouTube, in the not too distant future, when I get around to it.

Les, Liz, Marilyn, Bryn, Rob and Sam ready to play.

The Suspects

Ian Tawter *played by Les Hayes*
Liz Feelbetter *played by Liz Gallagher*
John Trayner *played by Rob Tollman*
Marilyn Mistrict *played by Marilyn Balkwill*
Paul Larner *played by Bryn Griffiths*
Jo Felloni *played by Sam Christian*
The Detective *played by Don Balkwill*
Written by Don Balkwill. All rights reserved

If this show had been performed a few years later after the 'Gavin and Stacey' TV series had started, I'm sure we could have had a 'Nessa' type character amongst the school girls who, when the body was discovered, spoke that immortal line, 'What's occuring?'. See opposite page, Pam Allinson?

The Butlitz School Outing Murder (July 2005)

Early in 2005, I was again approached by the Barry Soroptomists to put on a Murder Mystery in July of that year; this time with the proceeds going to the Presidents Charities. For this show, I used the same characters as the Larnings murder mystery, which was originally performed in 1998, but this time set it on a school outing. The school was called Butlitz, This was a nod to the Butlins holiday camp, that had once been situated close to where we were performing and which was now closed.

The outing was on the Barry steam train that we had used previously. Most of the audience got into the spirit of the occasion and dressed as either school children or teachers. As before the murder took place on the train and the investigation was held in the waiting room of the station. This time all the characters were played by members of Abergavenny Theatre Group. This was the first appearance in murder mystery for Les Hayes and Rob Tollman, who took part in many future productions. Liz Gallagher, who had appeared in the CADS pantomimes, had by now moved to Llangynidr and joined ATG, appeared as the School Matron. Sam Christian and Bryn Griffiths were also newcomers and performed brilliantly but the opportunity didn't present itself for further roles in MM. Then of course there was Marilyn, my wife, who played the gym mistress. Some of the audience dressed as school children and were very enthusiastic and rowdy. I think they were hoping that they would get a good spanking!

Some of the ladies loved the idea of being school girls again. Pam Allinson is right of centre wearing sunglasses.

SEX and the SILVER SURFERS

Cast in order of appearance

Announcer .... BRYN GRIFFITHS
Rebecca Lovechild .... HELEN GERAGHTY
Joan Wrinkleworth .... MARILYN BALKWILL
Wendy Witless .... LIZ GALLAGHER
Pete Pastover .... LES HAYES
Ben Hurley .... CHRIS GRAY
Rosalind Conway .... LOUISA CONNELLY
Salome Strippolli .... SUE CHRISTIAN
Hilda Coldtitz .... JANET RICHARDS
Dylis Pandy .... SAMANTHA CHRISTIAN
Ruper DeBear .... ROB TOLLMAN
Ernest Svine .... JOHN GERAGHTY
The Mole Catcher .... DON BALKWILL

Sex and the Silver Surfers was written by Don Balkwill & Jane Laurenti.

This production was adapted for sound recording and directed by Don Balkwill
and recorded at the Borough Theatre, Abergavenny on Saturday 30th July 2005.

Grateful thanks to Stage Manager, Ken Williams and Technical Manager, Dave Tulloch,
who were responsible for sound recording and effects.

Our thanks also go to Nick Banwell, Manager of the Borough Theatre,
to the Theatre Management Committee and to Monmouth County Council
for their support for the project.

Graphic design by Les at Hannibal Graphics email: les_hayes@mac.com

All proceeds from sales of this CD are used to support future productions.

Copyright of this production remains entirely with the author. The work may not be reproduced or broadcast in any other form or media without the express permission of the author.

Marilyn Balkwill, Liz Gallagher, Sam Chistian, Les Hayes, Chris Gray
and Sue Christian as residents of The Watershed.

CD recording of Sex and the Silver Surfers (July 2005)

The successful recording of 'Lies, Sex and Discotheques' led me into thinking about rewriting the 'Watershed' as a radio play. The theatre group members who took part in LS & D were all up for it. Once again, I wanted a more evocative name than the Watershed and it was Les Hayes who again came up with a great title 'Sex and the Silver Surfers'. They do say sex sells, and so it proved to be because we had a sizeable sexy audience, although to suggest they dress in basques was a bit extreme! I used the Watershed story but as with LS & D, added an announcer to set the scene and give verbal descriptions of the action where needed. If you read the earlier outline of 'The Watershed' you will remember, that the play is set in a retirement home for single people and their inept attempts to murder the new owner. We performed this play as part of the Abergavenny Festival in July 2005. It was recorded in The Abergavenny Borough Theatre, as before, but this time in front of a live, boisterous and paying audience. If you would like to listen to the play it might still be available on YouTube. An amusing story relating to both CDs. Across the road from where I worked was a 'Cardiff Institute for the Blind' shop, so after copies of both CD's had been produced I thought these would be great for their 'Talking Books' library. So, one lunchtime I went across the road with a copy of each CD to donate to them. I explained my intentions to the lady in the shop and handed over the CDs. She took one look at the titles and handed them back to me saying they were unsuitable. When I asked why she replied that they didn't want 'pornographic' items in their shop. I tried to explain that they weren't pornographic in any way, but were comedies and the titles were not indicative of the content. She did take them back but I could see she was dubious and I wouldn't be at all surprised if as soon as I left the shop they were thrown in the bin! Pity if all that fun and laughter went to waste.

Sex and the Silver Surfers

Sam as Dylis Pandy declares her innocence to Les who looks on aghast. Method acting from Les using a rollator for the recording of a radio play

Just for fun we used message boards to tell the audience when it was time to laugh. Not that they were needed of course!

Janet playing the Matron Hilda Coldtitz makes her presence felt.

"SEX AND THE SILVER SURFERS"

A LAUGHTER PACKED COMEDY SET IN A RETIREMENT HOME FOR SINGLE PEOPLE - "SEX AND THE SILVER SURFERS" IS AN ADAPTATION BY DON BALKWILL OF THE PLAY "THE WATERSHED" CO-WRITTEN BY HIM AND JANE LAURENTI, SOME SIX YEARS AGO, AND WHICH HAS BEEN PERFORMED IN A NUMBER OF VENUES THROUGHOUT SOUTH WALES AND EVEN ADAPTED AND STAGED IN TEXAS, USA.

MONDAY, AUGUST 01, 2005

The Radio play was successfully recorded by the Abergavenny Theatre Group in front of a somewhat troublesome but enthusiastic and lively audience.

ABOUT ME

GEORGINA LESTER
ABERGAVENNY,
MONMOUTHSHIRE,
UNITED KINGDOM
Business and marketing mentor/consultant specialising in online marketing.

Saturday 30th July quietly settled in the local theatre - well what can I say? What a night out! Giggle filled fun with lots of bawdry innuendos, pepperings of panto punch lines and vibrant contributions from a spirited, if sometimes rebellious audience. The recording of "Sex and the Silver Surfers" was an extremely successful evening. Set in a retirement home for single people where life is relatively quiet and undisturbed except for the occasions when we realise that the residents still have sex very much on the brain even if surfing the net is the only way they are going to get any. We know that their world is going to be turned upside down by the evil and greedy antics of the nephew of the owner of the home but how and what will cause the chaos we don't know.

The cardiganed and bespectacled geriatrics sporting various strangely quirky hats and head decor, gin bottles and twirling twinkly nipple tassels, tottered genteelly onto the stage. Supported by an array of mobility aids they delivered a torrent of naughty references, sexual promises, coupled with a shaky but honest admission that talking about it was all they were really up to in the twilight of their days in the home. However, wrinkles on the skin do not mean that there were wrinkles in the brain – their antics and devious plots were reminiscent of vibrant and energetic youth even though they occasionally lost the plot or got deaf or fell asleep or .....

A well timed joke, a good old fashioned cliché, many a play on words kept the audience laughing from beginning to end.

Review of the show from Georgina Lester, a local business person.

The fact that she was also a friend had no influence on her opinion whatsover!

Honest Guv!

39

Illustration DAMIEN O'FARRELL

The action takes place in the home of Martin and Margaret Duggan in the north of England

Act I	Scene 1:	December 23rd (evening)
	Scene 2:	Christmas Eve (morning)
	Scene 3:	Christmas Eve (evening)
Act II	Scene 1:	Christmas Day (morning)
	Scene 2:	Christmas Day (later)
	Scene 3:	Christmas Day (late afternoon, early evening)

SUPPORT FOR THE PRODUCTION PROVIDED BY:

Director	DON BALKWILL
Prompt	HAZEL GRAY
Stage Manager	KEN WILLIAMS
Sound/lighting	IOAN WYNN
Set design & construction	CHRIS GRAY
Makeup	SHIRLEY BARNFIELD
Wardrobe	ANOUSKA LESTER & FELICTY STEWART
Wardrobe consultant	JUDITH JONES
Props	HANNAH GETHING & HELEN GERAGHTY
Props consultants	JUDITH CANDLER & BRENDA DAVIES
Promotion & publicity	GEORGINA LESTER
Graphic design	LES HAYES

The Company's grateful thanks go to the Management and staff of the Borough Theatre Abergavenny for their continuing help and support.

CAST IN ORDER OF APPEARANCE

Goff	BRYN GRIFFITHS
Margaret	LIZ GALLAGHER
Helen	KIRSTY FLYNN
Martin	JOHN GERAGHTY
Fiona	DELLA MIDDLETON
Jimmy	ROB TOLLMAN
Chapman	LES HAYES
Monica	DEIDRE MAHON
Kathy	VIKKE CARTLEDGE
Crispin	TOM GIBSON
Pat	LIZ WATERS
Hughie	PAUL WATERS
Boy	BOBBY WATERS
Girl	HARRIET GERAGHTY

Comfort and Joy (Nov 2005)

The time had arrived for me give up acting in plays because I found I could no longer remember lines, I was fine with murder mystery events because that was all ad-lib. So, to be of use to the theatre group, it was time to try my hand at directing again. I chose, and the selection committee agreed, Mike Harding's 'Comfort and Joy' because it is a very funny comedy about the perils of Christmas. The play is set in the front room of Martin (John Geraghty) and Margaret (Liz Gallagher) Duggan who are looking forward to the visit of their two daughters Helen (Kirsty Flynn) and Kathy (Vikki Cartledge). The only trouble is, one daughter has a flatulent dog and the other has pooing cats, and guess what, they don't get on (the dog and cat not the sisters). Then there's Crispin (Tom Gibson), Kathy's bottom obsessed boyfriend and Margaret's Uncle Goff (Bryn Griffiths) a sprightly but irascible 70-year-old, who is staying with them for Christmas and is expecting a visit from his dim-witted daughter Fiona (Della Middleton), who he hasn't seen for 30 years; not since she ran off to Australia with Jimmy (Rob Tollman), a married, pop star look-alike from the local swimming baths. Add to this is a visit from their new 'Angel spotting' neighbours (Les Hayes & Dee Mahon), a couple of passing aliens (Harriet Geraghty & Bobby Waters – not actual aliens) and a very nice couple (Liz & Paul Waters) with a dark secret, and you had all the ingredients for an evening of mayhem and laughter. Mike Harding graciously allowed me to make whatever changes were needed to suit the local audience. It was a tremendous success and was one of the highest-grossing plays ever put on by Abergavenny Theatre Group with nearly 400 attending over the 3 nights. The play was performed on the 3rd to the 5th of November 2005.

Acting can be tiring, Vikki, Della, Liz, Kirsty, Bryn and Tom.

Scenes from Comfort and Joy

Della Middleton,sitting on the sofa, in her first role did very well but it was also her last with us because we never saw her again. I wonder what happened to her?

Dee Mahon and Les Hayes played the bonkers 'Angel spotting' neighbours too convincingly, which is why Bryn Griffiths as Uncle Goff, sitting in the middle, is looking on totally bemused

John Geraghty as Martin, listens aghast to Rob Tollman, as Jimmy, whilst Tom Gibson, as Bobby, gawps at Vikki Cartledge in her first role with ATG. She as Kathy, wonders who the hell has given her this dreadful, old fashioned nightdress.

The two Aliens that wern't, Bobby Waters & Harriet Geraghty

Liz Galagher in her first role for ATG won the Best Newcomer Award for her performance as the long suffering Margaret

Liz and Paul Waters as Pat And Hughie, the couple with a secret. The Waters appeared in a number of productions for ATG and went on to perform in a number of murder mystery events.

Having spent many months involved with the organising and directing of this show I found it very difficult with nothing to do during the performances.
I remember John Geraghty taking me to one side during the dress rehearsal and telling me not to interfere because my job was done. All I could do was sit in the dressing room, try and read a book, and wait. Very frustrating! I needn't have worried though, everybody was superb.

MEMORIES OF CHILDHOOD

Don Balkwill

GROWING UP AT CHAGFORD BRIDGE
1949—1981

MEMORIES OF CHILDHOOD   DON BALKWILL

MEMORIES OF CHILDHOOD

Britain during the 1950s: forward looking and taking advantage of all that modern technology has to offer – unless, that is, you're a family living in a two roomed shack on the edge of Dartmoor without gas, electricity or running water....

DON BALKWILL ...grew up in Devon. Within a short time of leaving school he moved to the RAF after which he settled in Wales where he now lives with his wife, Marilyn, in Abergavenny. He has written and performed in pantomimes, stage and radio plays. He currently writes and performs Murder Mystery evenings to raise money for his favourite charities and good causes. This is his second book.

Available from www.Memoriesof childhood.co.uk

44

Memories of Childhood (April 2006)

In the early part of 2006, I felt the urge... To be honest, back in those days, I felt all sorts of urges, but we won't go into that here. This one was to write a book about my early life growing up at Shaugh Bridge, on the edge of Dartmoor. At the time, I had three grand-daughters who were living a relatively affluent lifestyle. I thought it would be interesting for them, at some time in the future, to learn what my life was like growing up just after WW2, when we had very few material possessions and lived without basic amenities like electricity, gas, flush toilets, and running water. All of my grandparents had died before I was five years old, so I never had a chance to talk to them about their early lives. Likewise, with my parents I was never mature enough to be interested in their younger lives when they were still alive. But now I wish I had talked to them. So, that is what this book was for. If in the future the girls want to know about me it is all written down.

I decided, that I was going to self-publish the book because I didn't think that there would be sufficient interest from the wider public to make it worthwhile for a book publisher to take it on. As I've said, initially this book was to be exclusively for the grand-daughters, but as time went by, and because I had also created a website so that I could carry out research into the history of Shaugh, I found other people were interested in reading about my experiences. There was more demand than I had originally thought, so in the end, I had to have the book reprinted as the first print run sold out. What also helped the sales was that both Plymouth and Devon Library services liked the book and bought copies to distribute to all their branch libraries. At the time of writing this they are still available in their catalogues. Once again, I am indebted to Les Hayes who used his expertise to create the layout of the book.

To have a physical copy of my first published book made me not only very happy but also proud.

Above: Discussing the area with the interviewer
Below: Setting up for the shoot

Filming The Legendary Trail (June 2007)

As a result of my 'Parish of Shaugh' website, and the publicity received in the Devon local press for 'Memories of Childhood', I received a call from Encore Productions, which is a small film production company based in Plymouth. They were planning to make a series of DVDs on the many legends of Dartmoor. Because I had made mention of some of these legends on the website and in my book they asked me to take part (No I'm not one of those legends). So, in June 2007, I went back to Shaugh Bridge and my segment was filmed. Possibly, it can still be seen on YouTube. Just type in a search engine 'Legends of Dartmoor' and my name. It was recorded at the foot of the Dewerstone Rock, where I played as a boy. Sadly, as far as I'm aware, nothing ever came of the project, so I never made it to the big screen or the little screen for that matter. Ah well, another chance of fame had passed me by, but it was nice to be asked to take part and it was fun doing it.

Filming just about to start.

Murder at the Newoptimists (February 2008)

Somebody from the Barry Soroptomists had recommended our little group to the Newport branch of the Soroptomists, and they approached us to put on a Murder Mystery for them to help raise funds for Cancer Research (Cymru) in February 2008. I wrote a murder mystery based on a fictitious organisation called the Newoptomists (see the play on words?). We duly performed the show in the Newport Freemasons Hall, a very salubrious building, which we were given a guided tour of beforehand, but were asked not to take any photographs. (Form your own judgement about that!). The cast was made up of four members of ATG plus three volunteers from the Soroptomists. All went well and there were no secret handshakes or rolled up trouser legs to be seen all evening.

Annual Dinner of the Newoptomists
A group of people who prefer to look forward rather than back and also like to help people less fortunate than themselves.

Your committee and Guest as they appear on the top table facing you.

Chief Inspector Richard Head
Guest Speaker
Played by Don Balkwill

Luce Moralis
Committee member for 18 months. Nursing sister in the local Hospital.
Played by Louisajane Conte

Vernon Crook
Treasurer for last 12 months. Manages a chain of chemist shops.
Played by John Geraghty

Betty Diddit
Secretary of the Newoptomists . Process Supervisor in a local chemical plant.
Played by Christine Collingbourne

Juan Latiff
Committee member. Billionaire Argentinean businessman.
Played by Tony Tagg

Dr Bessie Mates
Committee member. Retired doctor but works as Hospital visitor.
Played by Pam Pugh

Carl Bigamister
Committee member. Owner of chemical manufacturing plant.
Played by Les Hayes

The Midshires Murder (Sept 2008)

In 2008 I was working for Birmingham Midshires in Cardiff as a Mortgage Underwriter. On the whole, it was a good place to work, because the powers that be did their best to engender a fun and pleasurable environment to while away the hours. The staff did lots of charity fundraising which was supported by the company. I suggested, and it was agreed by the management, that we could perform an in-house murder mystery to raise funds for Marie Curie Cancer Care. It turned out to be one of the more difficult shows to write and perform. To start with, the staff were spread over three floors of our office block. I had six work colleagues who volunteered to be suspects, two on each floor. I, in my persona as Inspector Donald Canard, co-ordinated the investigation and provided clues by email throughout the day to everybody in the building. Each department had its own detection team and appointed investigators who roamed the building finding the suspects and asking them questions. I called it 'The Midshires Murder' (well what else?). Of course, there were managers who complained that people were neglecting their workload to take part, but who wants to work when you can play at being detectives instead? Anyway, just a year later we were all made redundant.

Is Inspector Canard about to finger a suspect or is he testing which way the wind is blowing?

The Midshires Murder (September 2008)

Blood-curdling screams rang out from CMP on 30th September. This time it wasn't anything to do with TBDM Alex Creasy's choice of shirts...

Chief Inspector Richard "Don't call me Dick!" Head walked into the boardroom to find a terrible scene. Company boss "Big Ed" was found dead with six suspects who all bore striking resemblances to CMP staff.

Due to police funding cutbacks Inspector Head (played by the Midshires Murder creative force Don Balkwill) turned the sleuthing work over to BM Cardiff staff. CMP's sleuths then proceeded to mercilessly grill the six suspects throughout the day to get to the truth and also to discover which brand value the suspects represented.

The killer was finally identified as Jane "Bubbles" Bronson who was played by none other than HBOS Green Angel

In the grand tradition of Scooby-Doo she would have got away with it if it wasn't for you pesky kids...

Bubbles' motive was a crime of passion. A previous fling with Big Ed was about to come into the open and she couldn't risk losing out on her boyfriend's inheritance. Bubbles did what TCT is sure any of us would do in that situation and poisoned Big Ed by mixing strychnine into his artificial sweetener.

The winning team were presented with a Marie Curie Cake for their efforts in bringing such a nefarious killer to justice. Munching on said cake were mortgage-desk super-sleuths; Andrew Morris, Amy Williams, Lewis Richards, Amy Rees and Kris Lloyd. Thanks also to our other (innocent) suspects played by John Hogan, Jane

Paul-David and June O'Shea. The event raised £68.90 for Marie Curie which will be doubled with HBOS match funding. Many thanks to all who joined in.

Don's next Murder Mystery production is being performed in Abergavenny Borough Theatre on 7th and 8th November. Details on the poster in the Staff Room or direct from Don himself.

The winning team of Amy Williams, Lewis Richards and Amy Rees being presented the cake by me. Not in the picture is team Captain Kris Lloyd.

whodunnit?: Don Balkwill gets into character for Cardiff's murder mystery day

SCREAMS FROM CARDIFF

Murder mystery event raises money for Marie Curie

Screams have been ringing out from Cardiff as the BM fundraising murder mystery day took place.

Created by Cardiff Mortgage Processing's (CMP) Don Balkwill, colleagues used their super-sleuthing abilities to cross-examine each of the six suspects to identify the murderer and their methods. Colleagues also had to determine which brand value the suspects

represented. The winning team (Andrew Morris, Amy Williams, Lewis Richards, Amy Rees and Kris Lloyd) were presented with a Marie Curie cake for their efforts.

Don said: "I've been raising money for charity by writing and performing in Murder Mystery evenings for over 10 years. Having each suspect (with the exception of the murderer) represent a brand value, made the "Midshires Murders" one of the most interesting and unusual productions that I have undertaken."

The event raised £68.90 for Marie Curie, which will be doubled with HBOS match funding. Well done to everyone who took part in the event.

YOU SAY

"My team and I looked at all the clues and some things just didn't add up. We super sleuths came up with the motive and the murderer. We all enjoyed the event and enjoyed our winners' cake even more..." KRIS LLOYD, TEAM LEADER

Details of the event appeared in the BM company magazine in December 2008.

I keep telling you, if you point guns at people then somebody is bound to get hurt!
See below.

The Golden Gun Awards again (Oct 2008)

A repeat of the very successful Golden Gun Awards murder mystery, but this time for the NSPCC in Ponthir on 10th of October 2008. Yes, they had us back yet again! This was one of the funniest and most enjoyable performances of this show, due to the way Liz Waters as the matriarch, and Vikki Cartledge as the mistress sparked off against each other. Also worth mentioning is the performance of Sophie (Liz's daughter) as the murder victims daughter. This was her first performance for us, and sadly her last, because she went off to University soon afterwards. One of the highlights of this murder mystery is that after the murderer has been revealed the characters, with the exception of Don Cortesone, all end up dead because they shoot each other. This ending was so enjoyed by the audience (bloodthirsty lot) that it was incorporated into future performances of this show. Another great evening and over £600.00 was raised for the charity.

L to R: Me, Sophie Murray, Les Hayes, Vikki Cartledge, Rob Tollman,
Liz Waters and John Geraghty.

A ticket for the show only cost £7.50. What incredible value we were!.

53

Above:One of the most difficult things to achieve with so large a cast is getting them all on stage, another is keeping the them quiet whilst people are speaking their lines!

John Geraghty did an excellent job co-ordinating all the sound effects. John was another founding member of Dai Laughing Productions and is still taking part today.

At the after show party I was presented with a framed copy of the poster which had been signed by all the cast, I couldn't have asked for anything more.

Lies, Sex and Discotheques the stage play (Nov 2008)

In mid-2008, because ATG were having to postpone their play planned for November I was asked whether I could put on another radio play as a theatre production in its place, so that they would retain their autumn slot in the Borough Theatre's calender. I had already adapted 'The Mates Murder' from a stage play into a radio play, which we had recorded on CD in 2005, so it wasn't a major problem to turn it back into a stage play again but this time being performed as a radio play on stage - confusing or what? The reason for using this format was that we wouldn't need to build a set and the only props we required were microphones with stands to give the impression that we were recording a radio play in a studio. We gave two performances on the 7th and 8th of November 2008, and each night, we stopped the performance before the end to give the audience the opportunity of guessing the identity of the murderer and what their motives were for committing the dastardly deed.

On the first night, most of the cast from the original 1997 performance of 'The Mates Murder', Page 11, attended. (You may remember this play was adapted from the Mates Murder). At the after-show party, it was great fun for us all to meet up again and swap reminiscences.

Vikki Cartledge, Tony Tagg, Kayleigh Malsom put feeling into their parts, Les Hayes sitting, wonders what they're all going on about. All four became founder members of Dai Laughing Productions

INCLUDING OVER 250 PHOTOGRAPHS

THE BOOK OF

SHAUGH PARISH

It's a Shaugh Thing

DON BALKWILL

The front cover of my second published book A4 hardback

The Book of Shaugh Parish (Oct 2008)

If you have been paying attention and reading these pages in sequence, (if you haven't then smack yourself on the wrist), you may remember that my first book, 'Memories of Childhood' generated more interest than I had initially expected. So much so that people started sending me their memories of growing up in the area. As a result, I built up quite a portfolio of stories. Eventually, somebody on the Shaugh Prior Parish Council suggested I contact Halsgrove Publishing, who specialise in publishing non-fiction books with regional interest. After discussions with Halsgrove, they agreed to publish a 160-page hardback book in their communities history series. However, I needed more stories, so I began encouraging more people from the area to write down their stories and send them to me. In addition I was invited to take part in various community activities, where I recorded other peoples stories and memories and copied dozens of photographs. I made numerous visits to the Shaugh area and the surrounding villages. The book came out in October 2008. It had good reviews in the local press and by those who read it and contacted me. It also resulted in my being invited to talk about the book on local BBC radio in Devon, and eventually an invitation by the National Trust to open a new bridge at Shaugh... but more of that later. A number of copies were sponsored by the minerals company, Sibelco, who operated the local china clay works. Their copies of the book were donated to Plymouth and Exeter libraries.

Handover of books to Plymouth Library with Sibelco representatives

A BOOK OF SHAUGH PRIOR – *It's a Shaugh Thing* by Don Balkwill. Published by Halsgrove at £19.99. Hardback 160 pages. ISBN 978 1 84114 694 2

This book covers the villages of Shaugh Prior, Wotter and Lee Moor on the southern edge of Dartmoor.

It is unlike any of the other books in the Community History as about 50% of the book is based on the memories of people who lived and worked in the area. There are over 200 photographs of the three villages, many never published before. Shaugh Bridge, Shaugh Halt and the Dewerstone feature as does the china clay works at Lee Moor. Don has written a chapter about the pains of writing the book which is a great read and ends "What comes next I wonder? Shaugh the play? Shaugh the Movie?

As the author says this book is not meant to be the history of Shaugh but it is a loving, unashamedly nostalgic and pictorial tour. First class work, worth a read but then I visited the area with my parents when I was a child so I have always been attached to the place, well Shaugh Bridge and the woods nearby.

RATING: *****

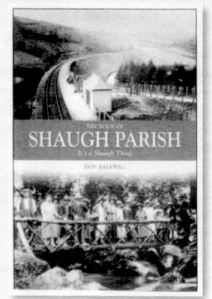

*Above
Review from
Dartmoor Magazine*

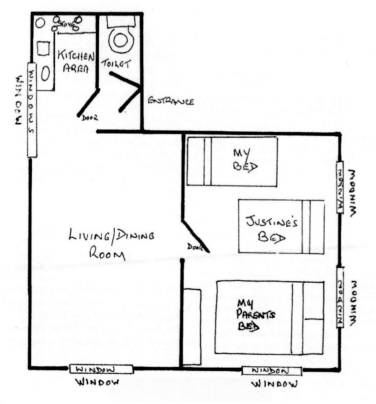

*Plan of the two room corrugated iron chalet that my family lived in for eleven years.
Drawn by c ,kChris Titchener.*

One of the proudest moments of my life was finding copies of my book on the shelves of the Plymouth branch of Waterstones.

The forming of Dai Laughing Productions (October 2009)

At a meeting of theatre group people who had already appeared in, or were interested in performing murder mysteries shows, it was suggested that we form a group, separate from ATG, who's sole aim was to raise funds for good causes by performing murder mystery events wherever they were required. Once again, Les Hayes came up with a brilliant name and so 'Dai Laughing Productions' was born.

The group reacted unexpectedly on being informed that Dai Laughing Productions had been formed.

Our Logo was designed by Les Hayes, who else?

Murder at the National Society for the Upkeep of Public Conveniences (March 2010)

One of the things that sparked the formation of Dai Laughing was that in 2009 I had been asked by Liz Waters, who had already appeared in a number of our murder mysteries, and who was the fundraising coordinator for Ty Hafan, whether we could put on a show to raise funds for her charity. Ty Hafan is a charity that provides support for children with life-shortening illnesses, so it was a no-brainer to agree to.

So, our first show as DLP was 'Murder at the NSUPC' (National Society for the Upkeep of Public Conveniences) which was performed in the King of Prussia in March 2010, for the benefit of Ty Hafan. Although we have had murders take place on stage in previous shows, this one was a bit different, in that the murder victim, in the form of David Haswell, (well known artist and amateur magician), performed a short magic routine beforehand, the highlight of which was appearing to remove one of the suspect's bra without her knowing about it, before he expired. One spooky little thing that Kayleigh Malsom, in her first MM, recalled from this show, was that during questioning she was asked by a member of the audience if she was pregnant with the murder victims child? She said no, but little did she know that she was actually expecting Brooke, her first! In fact, it was the next day she found out she was pregnant, so that was a little wild!

Not only did we provide the show, we did all the organisation of the venue, the meal, the promotion and the selling of the tickets. It was a lot of hard work, but over £1,500.00 was raised for Ty Hafan, one of our best ever results.

Can you guess my role? Andrea Hitchman as a Doctor from the audience, Les Hayes, Liz Waters, John Geraghty and Kayleigh Malsom

Murder at the National Society for the Upkeep of Public Conveniences.

I'd like to tell you it was all sweetness and light during our first show as Dai Laughing Productions but………………

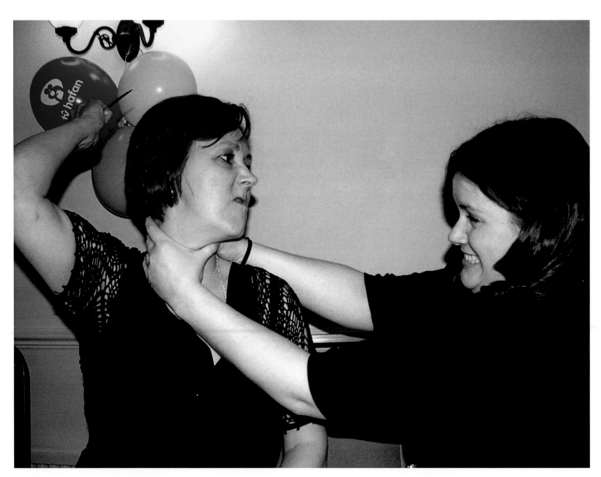

David Haswell finds an orange in Vikki's bosom, Most women make do with a handkerchief!

John reckoned that the Police need a hand to point them in the right direction.

63

Tony Tagg loves his Pussy

Les as the Dame holds another Dame, Vikki!

Liz, Les, me, Vikki, Tony, John and Kayleigh, the wacky bunch!

Cinderella, the sequel, becomes a Murder Mystery (Oct 2010)

'Flushed' with the success of our Public Conveniences murder mystery we decided to put on another one in 2010, this time for 'St David's Hospice Care'. The plot revolved around a provincial theatrical company performing a pantomime for the radio, 'Cinderella, the Sequel'. I took some of the scenes from the pantomime of the same name that Pam Allinson, and I had written back in 1998. Cinderella is now divorced, very rich, and living with her horrid stepmother again. Cinders wants another husband and is making every effort to find one. However, her stepmother is determined to foil her plans because she doesn't want to lose her meal ticket. She enlists the help of the wicked witch of Snow White fame. The witch uses the poisoned fruit ploy from Snow White, but instead of using an apple, decides to use a poisoned banana. Well, a banana is softer and slides down the throat easier. After eating the poisoned banana the actress playing Cinderella dies, and so the murder mystery investigation begins. Luckily, the actor playing the fairy godmother (me) is actually an undercover policeman who is investigating nefarious goings-on within the pantomime group. He takes control, and with the help of the audience, carries out the investigation there and then. Quite a simple plot really! The only downside of this show was, that nobody from St David's turned up. The venue was Llanfair Kilgeddin Village Hall which is a typical 1920s style green corrugated iron village hall; perfect for a pantomime themed show. Once again, our little group had organised everything. It was an awful lot of work but so worth it because it was a success. However, from then on, we decided to let the organisation we were performing for, do the booking of the venue and selling the tickets, whilst we would just provide the performance.

A few weeks later we hand over the cheque for St David's. Holding it is Kayleigh, John and Jenny Tagg, who was invaluable behind the scenes on numerous occasions

Elaine Smerdon & Gus Ferguson 'enthralled' as I talk about living at Shaugh Bridge

Re-creation of photograph taken over 30 years ago in the same spot.
Son Mark, Me, B in L Shaun, Sister Justine, Niece Sarah & Great nephew Ben who,
understandably, wasn't around at the time of the original

Opening the Bridge at Shaugh, twice (Nov 2010)

One of the proudest moments of my life was being asked to 'cut the ribbon' and declare open, a new bridge at Shaugh, where I grew up. Now, I know it was only a wooden pedestrian bridge, but it was a bridge nevertheless and I'm chuffed I was asked. I was contacted by Gus Ferguson, the representative of the National Trust and Head Ranger for South West Dartmoor, in September 2010, asking would I come down and open their new bridge over the Plym river at Shaugh Bridge. It appears I had been recommended to them by the Chairperson of Shaugh Prior Parish Council, Elaine Smerdon, because of the 'Parish of Shaugh' book that had been published in 2008. In fact, I opened the bridge twice! Why twice, you ask?. Well, at the allotted time, I cut the ribbon, did a, 'flowing', speech about the river and growing up in the area, and then led the crowd attending the opening across the new bridge. We were just about to retire to the village hall for tea and cakes when a press photographer turned up wanting to take photographs. He had been delayed and had difficulty in finding Shaugh Bridge. Well it is a small place. So, for the benefit of the press, I had to cut the ribbon again. Perhaps I should have felt twice as proud! Not only that but when, a couple of days later, an article was printed about the bridge opening in the Western Morning News, it was reported that I was 'a West country author and historian', not bad for a simple country boy who left school with no qualifications!

News

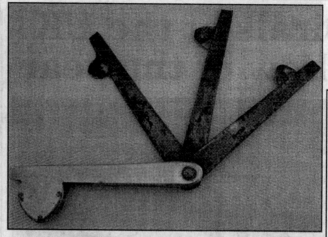

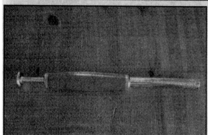

Were you able to identify last weeks object? A lot of people did.

This little gadget is called a "Kre-Mix Home cream maker" and was patented in 1933.

You stood it in a saucepan of hot milk mixed with butter, you then pumped the handle up and down like a bicycle tyre pump and hey presto in two or three minutes you have a rich pouring cream, or so the instruction leaflet tells you.

In it's day it cost 5 shillings and six pence in old money, the decimal equivalent of 27½ pence.

Using RPI the price today would be £14.50

As I said in my introduction last week, sometimes I will be featuring items that Grandma didn't use but nevertheless is a gadget, this weeks is one such. Three years ago somebody sent me a photograph of one of these items.

I had never seen or heard of it before but strangely enough a few weeks later whilst I was delving through a box of odds and sods being sold off by a market trader I came across one.

I recognised it straight away and bought it for a few pounds.

It looks something like a penknife with three blades and a brass handle.

The difference is that the "blades" are not sharp along the length however the protrusions from each of the blades are.

What do you think it was used for and do you know its name?

A clue; it had a quite gory use and was popular in the 17/1800's

Don't forget if you have any interesting gadgets you think our readers might find interested, or you need help in identifying an item, please feel free to either bring it to the Chronicle office or send in a photograph and I will endeavour to identify it for you,

If I am at a loss I will feature it in this column for, hopefully, our readers to identify.

If you have any comments or have personal experience of any of the gadgets featured please let us know

Above an early article without answer and below a later article with the answer.

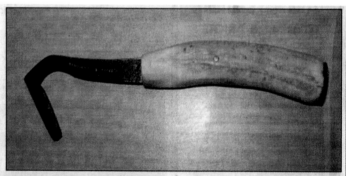

THIS week's object was shown to me by a Mrs. Dutson at a talk I gave quite some time ago, I haven't featured it before because this is the second time I will have written about one of these items, the reason for doing so again is because this one looks entirely different from the one originally featured.

This one is approximately 8 inches (20 cm) long and looks a bit like a knife with the blade bent over into a beak; the beak is spread into a channel or deep grove.

The handle is made of horn or antler and stamped on the blade is Townsend Hereford. Although I have been able to find others similar to this with the same name on the internet I've been unable to establish whether Townsend is the name of an individual or a company.

What do you think this was used for?

Answer

It is called a "Timber race knife" or a "Timber Scribe" and was used to mark numbers and symbols onto standing and felled timber.

The original one featured looked like a pocket knife with the blade folding into the handle.

The difference was that the blade had a folded over tip which formed the groove cutter. You use this type of knife for cutting a channel into the wood using the beak.

Early wood workers constructing oak beamed cottages would mark timbers so they knew where each beam was to be placed in the building.

These markings would be done using this type of race knife.

Forestry workers would mark the ends of felled timber so they knew who had bought the tree or where it was to go. Timber race knives are known to have been used on the shores of the Chesapeake Bay to scribe the waterline on wooden boats.

These knives have been around for many generations in various forms. You may wonder why it is called a "Race" knife. Well it is probably because "a race" can also mean "a channel". Gouging the knife along timber creates a channel in the wood so giving it its name. Did you guess what it was used for?

If you belong to an organisation that I've visited previously, I've put together my next batch of unusual objects for next year, so if you are looking to fill 2014's speakers calendar please get in touch again and I will be happy to oblige.

Keep bringing in, or sending photographs of your interesting gadgets.

Either take them to the Chronicle office or preferably send me a photograph by email. It doesn't matter if you don't know what it is because I will try to identify it for you. Your comments are always welcome so please contact me direct by email at memories@happyhome.plus.com

Grandma's Gadgets newspaper articles (Jan 2011-Nov 2017)

When I retired from paid employment in December 2010, I wondered what I was going to do to keep myself busy. I was still writing, and appearing in Murder Mysteries, but I felt I needed something more. I had been collecting old and unusual gadgets over the previous few years, with the aim of perhaps writing a book about them sometime in the future. I approached Liz Davies, the Editor of the Abergavenny Chronicle, and suggested, that she run an article each week, which I would write, featuring an unusual object, and ask the reader to guess what it was, before giving the answer the following week. Liz's response was that she liked the idea, but she couldn't pay me for contributing to the paper. It's a good job I wasn't looking for paid employment, wasn't it?

Sometimes, because of space limitations in the paper, the article was left out, so the poor reader didn't always get the answer to what the object was for a couple of weeks after it had first appeared. This annoyed some people, (and me), so I changed the format so that I not only asked the reader to guess what the object was ,but I gave them the answer later-on in the article. Writing the articles not only kept my mind active, but it also led me to write a book on gadgets in 2016. Another beneficial side effect was that various social and special interest groups began contacting me to ask me to give talks about forgotten gadgets to their organisations. But more of that a little later. 'Grandma's Gadgets', as the series was called was launched in December 2010 and appeared most weeks until 2017.

News

ABERGAVENNY CHRONICLE DECEMBER 9, 2010 PAGE 9

Edit
Fax:
Web.
www

The answers to your antique queries here in The Abergavenny Chronicle

HAVE you ever been to a car boot sale or antique fair and spotted an odd looking gadget or implement and wondered what it was used for?

Well if you have then you are going to have fun with this new series called Grandma's Gadgets which starts in The Chronicle in the New Year thanks to gadget expert Don Balkwill who has been collecting gadgets for many years.

Don says: "Over the last few years I have been categorising odd and the unusual gadgets and implements that people have discarded with the eventual aim of writing a book about them.

"It's always interested me how, throughout the ages, men and women have sought to make their lives easier by inventing gadgets to perform everyday tasks faster and more efficiently.

"You could say this started with the invention of the wheel however, the most prolific time has been the last 150 years.

"The changes in people's lives in that time have been enormous. The USA, which in the 1800s was a new and vibrant county, expanded at an incredible rate as go-getting people arrived to populate the country.

"They were the type of people who didn't sit back and let things happen, they made them happen. They wanted life to be quicker and easier so they invented the gadgets to make it happen.

"Here in Britain we have always had people who were leaders in inventing machines and structures that revolutionised industry all over the world. However it was the beginning of the 20th Century when the ruling classes began to reduce the number of servants in their households that an explosion of gadgets to help make household tasks less labour intensive happened.

"Some of these gadgets did make life easier, some were so complicated that they were rarely, if ever, used, others solved problems that didn't exist, many have been replaced by more efficient ways of getting the job done, some became obsolete because of modern production methods, and there were even those that were

downright dangerous," said Don.

"Each week I shall be bringing to your attention an item that fits into one of the preceding categories and you can have fun trying to guess what it is, or what it was used for.

"In many cases you will be able to view a short video of the item on the Chronicle website. The following week you will be provided with a history of the item,

assuming of course that I know what it is because in some cases I haven't been able to find out and I shall be asking for your assistance in helping me to identify it.

"In addition, if you have an item that baffles you and you would like it identified please either send in a photograph or if possible dropping it into the Chronicle office and I will be happy to try and find out what it is.

"Just to whet your appetite here are some objects for you to try and identify.

"As you can see they are all forks but can you guess what era they come from and what foods they were used with? For this week only the answers are provided here...

• All the forks are from the late 1800s to the early 1900s. The Victorians had a philosophy of designing cutlery to suit every different type of food to be eaten. From left to right they are.

• A bread or roll fork. Designed for time when it was frowned on to touch food by hand. Usually three tined, as this one is, they were fairly short up to about 17 cm (6 ½ inches) in length.

• A sardine fork. The design of a typical sardine fork was flat with numerous tines to provide horizontal support to keep the sardine in one piece until it reached your mouth. Up to about 13 cm (6 inches) in length.

• Fruit or berry fork. Either two or three tined they usually came as a set with a knife and were just the thing for your plate of strawberries.

All the forks were usually either solid silver or as these are silver plated. The handles are a popular material for the period, mother of pearl. All are very collectable but don't cost a fortune to buy.

SOUTH WALES

Argus

South Gwent
Children's Foundation
Registered Charity No: 1093690

sparkle

helpu plant arbennig i disgleirio
helping special children shine

www.thisisgwent.co.uk   Friday, March 4, 2011   Est. 1892   42P

BRITIAN'S FASTEST GROWING EVENING NEWSPAPER OVER 11 YEARS

BREAKING NEWS: Famous TV Presenter and Restaurateur Found Dead in Local Newport Hotel.........

We received breaking news that the well known TV presenter, Robert Burns-Waters, was found dead in his room this morning. Sources from the Hotel tell us that the death was not from natural causes however at this stage no further details are being released. Readers will know Mr Burns-Waters from his television series "Robert Rates Rubbish Restaurants" in which he tours the British Isles carrying out undercover checks on the hygiene and service standards of restau-

competition was to have been that exuberant and eccentric food writer, critic, and broadcaster, Delia Jones, who made her name when chosen to head up the TV cookery programme "Jones Junks food" which showed people how to cook similar the meals to those provided by fast food outlets but without all the fats, sugars, and additives.

The other judges of the competition were to have been Basil Mugwort, the retired restaurateur and raconteur. Another fellow

would have been in competition with Angus Bull, who has a chain of 3 Brasserie style restaurants in town centres dotted around South Wales Although he has a Scottish sounding name he

NEWS INSIDE

Firefighter off to quake zone

A Newport based firefighter is today set to land in the New Zealand earthquake zone, part of a rescue team of 55 from the UK.

- Full story: page 9

Swim star in Cup

Murder on the Menu! (March 2011)

Our next murder mystery was for the Sparkle appeal, which raised funds to build and run the Serennu Children's Centre situated just outside Newport. The Centre provides support for disabled children, young people, and their families. We were asked to perform the murder mystery on a Friday, during the day, so a number of our regular performers were unable to take part due to work commitments. However, we did recruit some new players, namely, Laura Collins, Pam Bush, Angela Brinkworth and Rob Gotobed, all of whom fitted in seamlessly. The plot of 'Murder on the Menu' is that the Sparkle Appeal Committee are hosting a celebrity chef cookery competition but one of the judges gets murdered. So... when the invited audience turned up they were initially unaware that this was a murder mystery event and not a cookery competition and it took them a while to get into the swing of things. The 'Celebrity chef contestants' and the 'Judges', already in character, were seated with the audience at different tables around the room. They were so convincing that some members of the audience tried to book reservations at their fictitious restaurants! As Laura, performing as one of the chefs, Sally Mollena, said: "The audience was slightly bemused by the whole thing but I managed to convince a male member of the audience that "I REALLY" did run a restaurant based in Skenfrith, which served up poultry dishes only ('Poultry, as in game birds, not paltry as in small, loike'). Bless Sally, she was a Cockney and strangled all her vowels - as well as her birds, probably... I was there as the world-famous, gourmet chef and detective, Monsieur Donald Canard, so I spoke 'Franglais' to the ladies on my table, and for a time I had them convinced I was French! The South Wales Argus even printed a fictitious front page, which we had composed, of their newspaper, announcing the death of the murder victim. Once things warmed up and the audience realised what was going on, it was a brilliant afternoon.

The show was performed at the Hilton Hotel, Newport on 4th March 2011.

Back row:Tony Tagg, Les Hayes et Moi

Middle: Laura Collins

Front row: Pam Bush, Rob Gotobed & Angela Brinkworth

DAI LAUGHING PRODUCTIONS PRESENTS

MURDER
on the
MENU

THERE'S MORE THAN FOOD ON THE MENU AT THIS YEAR'S WELSH HEATS OF "TRADITIONAL CHEF OF THE YEAR"...

Join us at The King of Prussia at 7.30pm on Saturday 5th March 2011 for dinner and an evening of homicidal hilarity designed to test your investigative powers of deduction and leave you with a smile on your face.

Tickets, £16.00 including a three course dinner, are available here and proceeds from the evening's entertainment are going to support the continuing work of Tŷ Hafan.

ty hafan
the family hospice
for young lives

Supporting Tŷ Hafan will make a real difference to the life-limited children, young people and their families who use our unique and vital services. For more information on fundraising for Tŷ Hafan or how to become a volunteer, please visit www.tyhafan.org/get-involved/start-fundraising Because you care, so can we.

A Charitable Company Limited by Guarantee Registered in Wales,
Registered Number 3077406 Registered Office: St Hilary Court, Copthorne Way, Culverhouse Cross CARDIFF CF5 6ES

Murder on the Menu (2) (also March 2011)

Do you remember that back in March 2010, we had performed a murder mystery in the King of Prussia? Well, the landlords, Jeff and Richard, were so impressed, that they asked us if they could hire us to put a show for them. We agreed on the proviso that our fee of £500.00 was donated to a charity, and this should be shown in the publicity. We again chose Ty Hafan as the beneficiary. The date was to be Saturday 5th March, the day after the show for Sparkle in Newport, so, it made sense that we use the same theme. In this show, we reverted to our usual format of having the suspects seated at a top table throughout the performance. Two of the cast were changed, Martin Crandon, another newbie, and John Geraghty a veteran of many shows, replaced two of the characters. Overall this made little difference to the performance. However, this audience was more proactive and responsive than the previous day's crowd. I think this was because they were expecting, and had paid for, a murder mystery event. Their enthusiasm rubbed off on the performers which meant that a thoroughly good time was had by all.

On the right the Chef Contestants, John Geraghty, Les Hayes and Laura Collins prepare to hone their cookery skills

Left: Moi, being pretentious and cultivating one of my moustaches

Meanwhile, the Celebrity Judges hone their wine tasting skills.

Both Pam Bush and Angela Brinkworth were professional actors in their younger days, and not to be left out, Martin Crandon took part in, and won, a number of prizes in amateur drama competitions when he was a young man.

L to R. Kayleigh Malsom's arm. Les Hayes. Laura Collins, Chris Broome, Angela Brinkworth and John Geraghty.

A member of the audience decided to get up close and personal with his questioning.

The Golden Gun Awards again (May 2011)

We were asked by 'St David's Hospice Care' to put on another murder mystery for them, but this time they would organise the venue and sale of tickets. I think the reason for this was because the hierarchy of the organisation felt a little guilty that none of their people had attended the Cinderella murder mystery that we had performed for them in the previous October. We even had Chris Broome, the Fundraising Manager for St David's, roped in as one of the cast. The show took place on 7th May 2011 at the Royal British Legion club in Usk. Because it had been so successful in the past, we again used the format of The Golden Gun Awards as the theme. Most of the audience threw themselves into the spirit of the occasion and dressed as gangsters or molls from the 1920s. Everybody was very enthusiastic throughout the evening, and they all thoroughly enjoyed themselves. Sorry about the quality of the photographs but these are the best of a bad group that were all out of focus, I think the photographer had a bad case of the shakes from laughing so much. At least that's my story and I'm sticking to it!

Everybody looking red, flushed and out of focus and not from drink either!

In an effort to make the evening as realistic as possible the meal supplied was reflective of the times in which the show was set. However, the coffee wasn't made from acorns!

Murder on the Peace Committee (Nov 2011)

The success of 'Murder on the Menu' performed in the King of Prussia prompted the owners to ask us back again, this time on Saturday 12th November 2011. This date was just after Armistice Day, and as the following day was Remembrance Sunday we decided it would be appropriate if we donated our fee to 'Help for Heroes'. The murder mystery would have a vaguely Military/Dad's Army theme. I set it in the fictitious town of Cwmbyeyer in 1945. The story revolved around a committee set up to plan the peace, but unfortunately, somebody decided to take the opportunity to bump off the Chairperson. We had well-known wartime music playing in the background throughout, and on two occasions during the evening the audience spontaneously broke out into song. Some of the costumes used by the cast were genuine WW2 outfits which we obtained from the Theatrical Costumiers 'ACE ' who, because this was a charity event, supplied them for a nominal fee. As you are no doubt aware, back in 1940's, due to rationing, people were a lot slimmer than today, which suited Laura, but not me, that is why I had to leave my uniform top open throughout the performance. I also had to have a gusset sewn into the back of the trousers! I still maintain that it was due to water retention although there could have been some 'beer' retention as well I suppose. We raised over £500.00 for Help for Heroes.

Back L to R: Me, Tony Tagg, Les Hayes, John Geraghty, Front: Vikki Cartledge, Laura Collins and Angela Brinkworth all looking the part

John as the Black Marketeer can get you anything you like!

Les makes a good Vicar, he's so pious!

A peaceful murder for charity

OVER £500 was raised for "Help for Heroes" when a Murder Mystery evening, "Murder on the Peace Committee" was held at the King of Prussia recently.

Because the chosen charity was "Help for heroes" it was felt to have an event with a sort of Dad's Army theme would be most appropriate.

So the mystery was set in the fictitious town of Cwmbyeyer in 1945 at the end of WW2 when a Peace Committee was formed to formulate plans to get the town back to normal after the tribulations of the war.

Unfortunately just after the meeting of the Peace Committee had started the Chairperson, Marianne DuBois, had a convulsion and died.

Major Grey, who had just arrived, took charge. His purpose there was to meet with Marianne because she was working for him as an undercover operative.

Her objective was to keep an eye open for possible spies and subversive elements in the town. Marianne was French and when the

war broke out and France was occupied she began working alongside undercover forces for the resistance in France.

She escaped to Britain when her resistance group was betrayed. It was suspected that one on the Peace Committee had poisoned Marianne so Major Grey, with the assistance of the audience, carried out an inves-

tigation there and then.

The suspects were Captain of the Home Guard Played by Tony Tagg, the Vicar played by Les Hayes, the Blackmarketeer played by John Geraghty, the Matron of Breville Hall Hospital played by Vikki Cartledge, the WVS Co-ordinator played by Laura Collins and the Lady of the Manor played

by Angela Brinkwater.

Major Gray was played by Don Balkwill who also wrote the Murder Mystery.

There were a number of very inventive solutions put forward but the mystery was eventually solved and the guilty party revealed.

An enjoyable evening was had by all.

The exotic sounding Marianne DuBois was the murder victim in this tale of spies and nefarious goings on, as told to the audience and then the Abergavenny Chronicle.

In a packed room we had a very attentive and enthusiastic audience.

The suspects were 'dying' of thirst. John, Vikki, Tony, below Pam, Les and an irate Angela

Murder, it's just not Cricket (March 2012)

In late 2011, I was contacted by a Jenny Jones, who had attended one of our previous Murder mysteries, she asked if we would be prepared to put on a show to help raise funds for Llanarth Cricket Club. As we considered this local club to be a good cause we agreed and used a cricket theme for the show. The setting was a pre-season dinner that had been organised by the new president of the cricket club. Unfortunately he was on a sticky wicket, as he got hit for six and was bumped off whilst making his welcoming speech. I bowled in and took over in the persona of William (Old Bill) Grace who was an administrator from the English Cricket Board and an ex-policeman. An enthusiastic and com-bat-ative audience helped to make this a great match between the audience and the performers. The murder victim was played by the actual Chairman of the Llanarth Cricket club, Keith Spencer, and the show was performed in the Park Hotel, Pandy just outside Abergavenny. I was bowled over to receive a very positive email from Jenny the following morning. "Good Morning Don, we have received no end of phone calls this morning from our guests last night, saying how much they enjoyed the murder mystery, and they want to do another one. Most of the feedback received, said, as actors, you were a very talented group of people, which I totally agree with. Please pass these messages over to your very 'talented friends'. In the process of entertaining this group, we helped them raise £470.00 in profit for the club. Howzat! for a winning result all round!

All the suspects look on aghast as the Chairman expires perhaps, somebody should have told them that to have a murder mystery you have to have a murder victim!

St Teilo's was jam-packed. Perhaps the way to get more people to attend church regularly is to stage a murder on a frequent basis, a fictitious one of course.!

Who killed Sir William Pertholey? (Sept 2012)

St. Teilo's, is a small but beautiful 12th-century church in Llantilio Pertholey on the edge of the village of Mardy, just outside Abergavenny. Various social events are held in the church to raise funds towards the upkeep and maintenance of the building and its surroundings. After attending one of these events, I suggested to our friends Verley and Les Toyah, who are involved with the church, that Dai Laughing could stage a murder mystery in the church. After discussions with the PCC and the Vicar, this was enthusiastically agreed to, so I set about writing a murder mystery with a medieval theme to suit the surroundings.

After initially struggling to bring the story together, it all fell into place after a brainstorming session with the cast at a local pub. They do say alcohol lubricates the brain, don't they? Set in the year 1312, we didn't have to worry about fingerprints or DNA on the murder weapon, so we had the victim, Sir William Pertholey, bludgeoned to death with a candlestick. Of course, we couldn't have this happen in the church, so we had him found in the graveyard. After all, that is normally where you find dead bodies, isn't it? The show was a rip-roaring success, raising over £800.00 for the church, and everybody enjoyed it. Incidentally, the ladies from the church made the monks costumes, and another friend, David Lucas, made the wooden crosses.

Pam Bush as Lady Pertholey puts her case very forcefully although Father Dinias looks decidedly unimpressed.
The cast L to R. Me, Vikki, John, Tony, Pam, Les, and Laura.

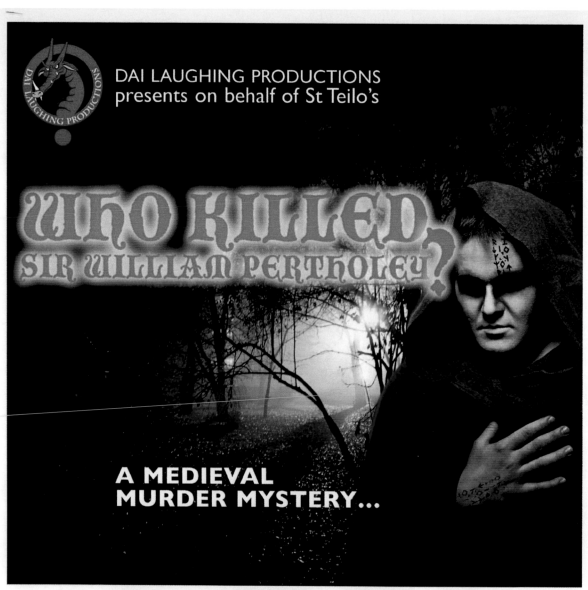

DAI LAUGHING PRODUCTIONS
presents on behalf of St Teilo's

WHO KILLED
SIR WILLIAM PERTHOLEY?

A MEDIEVAL
MURDER MYSTERY...

When the body of the Lord of the Manor Sir William turns up done to death and with the letter 'J' scrawled in blood by the battered remains, dark and tangled tales emerge!

CAN YOU SOLVE THE MARDY MEDIEVAL MURDER MYSTERY AND WORK OUT WHO BROUGHT THIS FILTHY KNIGHT TO AN EARLY CLOSE?

Trim your lanterns, secure your place and gather in St. Teilo's Church, Llantilio Pertholey (Mardy) before 7.30pm on

SATURDAY 22ND SEPTEMBER 2012

A tarriff of £15 will include supper victuals and fruit of the vine. To purchase your tickets please call 01873 858235

A suitably atmospheric poster designed by Les Hayes. What a talented man!

84

Back: A butcher, Investigating priest, Victim's younger brother.
Front: Nun, (sister to victim), Village priest, Lady of the Manor, M'lady's maid.

John Geraghty in his smartest acting togs

Laura Collins giving forth like only Laura can

Vikki Cartledge was asked to leave the Convent because of her dirty habits!

Les Hayes looks smug because he thinks he will inherit the estates

Tony Tagg as the village priest fears he will lose his stipend

Pam Bush as Lady Pertholey fears she will lose everything

Who killed Sir William Pertholey? (2) (Sept 2012)

Due to the success of previous performances for NSPCC, Ponthir branch, we had been booked to put on another murder mystery for them one week after the show for St Teilo's church, so it made sense to repeat the same show with the same cast. Once again, this was in Ponthir Village Hall, which has a very small stage, This made it a bit difficult for the suspects to have the histrionics that they usually do, but they managed it magnificently. That's actors for you!. A few days later we received a letter of thanks from the organisers telling us that the performance had been another success raising £677.00 for the NSPCC. Not only that, but we also recruited another performer from the audience, Margaret Barrell, who was to appear in a number of our future productions.

Below: It was all a bit cramped but we managed it, even I got a clap at the end!

*Whilst giving his speech poor old Tony had to contend with a pillar right in front of him.
Not only that but his death scene was also obscured from a number of the audience*

*Inside Pam's walking stick is a glass phial which could contain the poison, but does it?
Rob Tollman played Glen Green the Groundsman, and no, the beard's not real*

Murder to a Tee (April 2013)

As a result of the success of the various shows we had performed for NSPCC in Ponthir, we were contacted by Blaina and District NSPCC and asked to perform a murder mystery for them. This we did on Saturday 27th April 2013 at the West Mon Golf Club, which is the highest golf club in the UK. I'm told that part of the golfer's dress code up there is mittens and earmuffs! I wouldn't be surprised if that was true, because it was very chilly up there, and this was in April. As you can see from the title, this was another show written especially to suit the venue. Margaret Barrell, who we had recruited at the last Ponthir show, made her debut and was excellent. The plot for this show entailed the President of the Golf club, Chip Hookshot, played by Tony Tagg, being poisoned at a dinner, which he had organised. It certainly raised a laugh when after he had 'died' and the cast members were trying to carry him off, Chip, unexpectedly, came back to life to help them. He walked off in the sight of the audience! The liveliest corpse you've ever seen. All the cast were tremendous as usual, but, worthy of special mention, is Rob Tollman, whose makeup was outstanding. Looking at him you wouldn't think he was a teacher, would you?

All in all, it was a tremendous success and it raised £620.00 for the charity.

John Geraghty, Pam Bush, Tony Tagg, Margaret Barrell, Rob Tollman, Les Hayes, Vikki Cartledge and Me

Margaret in her first show with Dai Laughing certainly played her role with some gusto!

Laura looks on in shock as Rob gives away her secret recipe for Duck Rillettes.

Both Carmela and Martin demonstrate their Tommy Cooper impressions.

Murder a la Carte (May 2013)

In Abergavenny, there is a very active Alzheimer's Society support group, and a number of their members had attended previous murder mystery events. So we were asked if we would put on a show for them. This we did, on Saturday 11th May 2013, in the Llanfoist Village Hall (No we didn't forget to turn up (a joke in bad taste)). The setting requested was a French restaurant so this provided us with an opportunity to revive our celebrity chef competition theme which had been so successful in previous performances. All we needed to do was change the title to give it a more French sounding title. We had four changes in the cast, two newcomers who were acting for the first time, Alan Clouth and Carmela Gianfagna. Everybody performed superbly. The hall was decorated, to look like a French Restaurant, by the members of the Society, and many of the audience dressed up in French costume. As in all of our murder mysteries, we ask the audience to name who they think the killer is and what they think the motive was before we reveal his or her name. Unbeknown to us, there was a real detective in the audience, and no, he didn't pick out the guilty party.... but his wife did! The evening was a tremendous success, so much so that £1,360.00 was raised for the Alzheimer's Society. Now that's what I call a result.

Back: Alan Clouth, Vikki Cartledge, Martin Crandon, and me giving a hand (note the tash)
Front: Laura Collins, Rob Tollman and Carmela Gianfagna.

I only wish I could remember all the names of the characters but most escape me, the ones I do remember are Rosemary Nettles played by Vikki and Sal Monella played by Laura.

Note than my moustache is different from the one on the previous page I often changed moustache mid performance just to see if the audience spotted it and made comment. Nobody ever did. Fine bunch of detectives they were!

Alan Clouth did a fine job in his first role in murder mystery considering he had no previous experience of acting.

Sal Monella was an unfortunate name for Laura to have in her role as a chef who specialised in poultry dishes

Chef's excuses for his flat Yorkshire puds didn't go down well with either of the judges.

I did offer to give Rosemary Nettles a hand with writing her book but she declined on the grounds I was a meat eating fascist pig. Ce qui Moi?

Rob Tollman took over the role of the pig-sticking bloodthirsty butcher. (typecasting) and John became the village priest. It was an age thing.

Vikki as the Nun looks longingly at the bread stick.

Laura who has become Lady Pertholey berates Marie-Anne playing Jennifer the maid, who Laura played in previous performances of this show.

Les just can't keep up with all these changes of personalities.

John as the local priest muses on his chances of staying in post when the new Lord of the Manor takes office. After listening to him Laura as Lady Pertholey wonders whether the power of prayer is powerful enough to help her keep her fortune. She will try anything!

Who killed Sir William Pertholey, again! (July 2013)

As you may already know I have been a speaker on Forgotten Gadgets to lots of local organisations, one such was Gilwern W.I. During the introduction to the talk I had told them about Dai Laughing and how we raised funds for good causes. As a result of this, we were asked to put on a show to help raise funds towards the refurbishment of St Elli's Parish Church, Llanelly. This is a very old church. People have been worshipping there since the 14th century or possibly even earlier, We duly did this on 12th July 2014, but at Gilwern Parish Centre, because the church was unsuitable for a show such as ours. Even though we were not in the actual church we thought it appropriate that we perform our medieval murder mystery again. We had to jiggle the cast around a bit. Laura took on the role of the murder victim's wife, Lady Justina Pertholey, and we brought in Marie-Anne Gibson to play the Lady's maid, Jennifer. This was Marie-Anne's first, but certainly not her last, murder mystery. John took over the village priest role and Rob stepped in as the butcher. The centre was jampacked, the audience asked some clever questions but, only one team had the correct solution. Feedback was that everybody enjoyed the evening, and £547.00 profit was made. One of my favourite pictures from that evening is of Vikki Cartledge dressed as the nun, Sister Joan, with a church banner behind her, which makes it look as if she has a halo. Vikki looking saintly and angelic, enough said?

Father Dinias had to use paper to keep a track of the clues unfortunately, we couldn't afford parchment or vellum.

Vikki, as the Nun, is not looking ethereal and out of focus because she has been sniffing the herbs. It was probably the photographer shaking because they thought they were having a mystical experience.

Les as Miles Moore, the Producer, Marie-Anne as Cinderella with the Wicked Witch, banana at the ready, played by John, I've got my black wig and best sparkly frock on as the Fairy Godmother, trouble is I look more like a drag queen than a fairy!

Everybody plays multiple parts in this show. Firstly, we as a murder mystery group are playing a fictitious theatre group, who are performing a pantomime. Marie-Anne not only played Fiona Goodbody who plays Cinderella but she also plays Polly Perfect the stage manager. I, as Rees Lewis play the Fairy Godmother and Lewis Rees the detective. Confused? The audience were and so were we!

Cinderella, the Sequel, again (Sept 2013)

How we came to be doing a murder mystery on a Saturday night in a green corrugated iron village hall, in Herefordshire in September 2013, I can't remember. I do know, that it was to help raise funds for Garway Church and Garway Primary School PTA. The hall itself seemed to be little changed from when it was built in the 1920's so it was perfectly suited to putting on a show with a pantomime theme. Which is why we decided to use "Cinderella, the Sequel" again. I expect over the years there have been many other shows performed in this hall but never one quite like this. This murder mystery is probably unique in that after the murder victim, Fiona Goodbody, a.k.a. Cinderella, dies the actor playing that part, Mari-Anne, reappears as the assistant stage manager, Polly Perfect, who turns out to be the twin sister of the murder victim and is also the murderer. Confusing or what? Oh! and we had the banana scene again! What a night we had - it was hilarious! At one point I was a bit concerned that we weren't getting enough questions from the audience, but as the evening wore on they really got into it. Maybe alcohol had something to do with it!

That doesn't matter. What matters is that the evening raised £720.00 to be shared between the two organisations.

The hairless Fairy Godmother with the rest of the cast listen disbelievingly to Candy Sweet as Dandini trotting out her excuses.

Garway Village Hall built in the 1920's

Sorry folks not the most flattering of photos but it was the best I could find.

Above: Our Les

Above: Margot meditating.

Left: Laura, usually not one to avoid the limelight.

Right: Alan, looking a bit fuzzy

Below: Rob being hairy

Below: First timer Judith

Murder on the Menu, again (Oct 2013)

Alan Clouth who appeared in "Murder a la Carte" in May was a supporter of VSO (Voluntary Services Overseas). He asked if we could perform the same show to raise funds for VSO, so of course, we agreed. This took place in the Holy Trinity Church Hall in Abergavenny whilst they were holding a Community Canteen session on Saturday 19th October 2013. Abergavenny Community Canteen hosts a cook-in once a month, bringing together local people who enjoy cooking and eating vegetarian meals. It raises money for a range of different causes and celebrates the cooking of different countries and regions. It also provides meals for people in reduced circumstances. Three supporters of VSO, including Alan, took parts in the show, Margot Seabourne and Judith Negus all did an excellent job. Having said that the all-round performance of the whole cast was outstanding. Some of the off-the-cuff jokes, puns and answers to questions from the experienced players, Laura, Rob and Les were really quite brilliant. The audience was responsive and all those who gave feedback said how much they had enjoyed it. The only downside for me was the small amount of money raised for VSO, only £300.00, but this was due to the way the Community Canteen charge for their meals, with no set ticket price. The diners pay what they want. Ah well, never mind we provided an excellent show.

As you can see Rob really enjoyed the vegetarian meal!

Vikki as Dandini again

Me as the Fairy again! Anne-Marie (Linda Goodbody) as
Cinderella and Les as Miles Moore (Wicked Stepmother)

Anne-Marie, John, Banana and two plums

Tom as (Harrison Bridge) Buttons and Margaret as (Deborah Delight) Prince Valentino.

Cinderella, the Sequel 3 (Nov 2013)

One of the advantages of our method of putting on a murder mystery is that it is very simple. The performers only have to learn who they are, where they fit in the scenario, and what dark secrets they need to reveal about the other suspects. These 'clues' are disclosed at the appropriate time throughout the show to divert suspicion away from themselves. (Trade secret, they usually have these disclosures printed on a piece of paper on the table in front of them, but the audience can't see that). Everything else is ad-lib. What this means is that we can slot replacement performers into a show almost seamlessly and at very short notice, although they do have to be the type of person who can think on their feet. Even though we had performed this MM less than six weeks previously we had to replace two of the cast. Tom Gibson made his debut as Buttons and Margaret Barrell, as Principal boy, made her second appearance. I'm assured Mari-Anne still enjoys bananas! We performed this for Abergavenny Rotary who were raising funds for the RP Fighting Blindness charity. It took place on Saturday 2nd November in West Mon Golf Club. It was great fun even though the layout of the venue caused a few problems. The audience was very raucous but really got into the spirit of the evening. £250.00 was raised from the sale of the tickets which was then matched by Rotary giving a total of £500.00 donated to the charity.

L to R. Back: Margaret, Les, John and me
Front: Vikki, Tom and Marie-Anne now as Polly Perfect

It's Murder at The Chron as the detectives are called in

IF you fancy a welcome break from stirring the Christmas pud or steaming the sprouts then why not take a trip to the Abergavenny Chronicle offices on Saturday, December 14 where the lid will be lifted on the sordid goings on behind the sedate doors of Nevill Street.

Join the Chronicle's new 'editor' Vi Lente and chief reporter Ed Lines as they team up with world famous detective Monsieur Donald Canard, to investigate the murder of newly appointed general manager Hugh B'Stard...or save themselves from being unveiled as the dastardly murderers!

The evening of murder, mystery and mayhem is being specially written and staged for the Chronicle by popular local group Dai Laughing and will raise funds for a national charity being supported by Tindle Newspapers in the coming year.

"The story line revolves around the appointment of a new general manager and the consternation that causes for the existing employees because in one way or another they all have something to hide and the new GM knows too much. So much so that some of them resort to the ultimate sanction," said Don Balkwill of Dai Laughing.

"To protect the innocent we have metaphorically sacked all the existing staff and replaced them with totally fictitious characters, we wouldn't want readers to believe that anybody working for the Chronicle could be as underhand and suspicious as characters, like Hugh B'Stard, Vi Lente, Callum Inches, Ed Lines, Pru Freeder, Nick Arsene and Paige Free.

"Fortuitously the famous French Crime writer and Detective Monsieur Donald Canard is on hand to take control when a murder takes place. As he himself says "Unfortunately like my friend Hercule, it 'appens that deaths occur wherever I am around, I don't understand why zis is but it 'appens and so I am called upon to solve yet anozer mystery".

To make the evening more exciting the event will take place in a luxury marquee situated in the Chronicle's secret garden and the £15 ticket price will include a two course fish and chip supper (bring your own wine) and a glass of bubbly on arrival.

Tickets are available now by ringing the Chronicle on 01873 852187 or by calling in to the Nevill Street office. So if you enjoy a murder mystery and think you have the skills needed to work out who did the dirty deed whilst having a laughter filled evening then hurry because space is limited.

It's Murder at the Chron (Dec 2013)

This was our seventh performance of 2013 and it was a real mystery to begin with because we didn't know which charity we were performing it for, This wasn't disclosed until the very last moment. Some months previously, Liz Davies, the Editor of our local newspaper the 'Abergavenny Chronicle' had asked if we would put on a MM for them in a marquee being erected at the back of the Chronicle's offices in Nevill Street. Liz said she couldn't tell us who we were performing for because she had been sworn to secrecy but all would become clear when the day of the event arrived. All we knew was that it was to support an, as yet, unnamed charity being supported by the owners of the Tindle Group who publish the Chronicle. I set about writing "It's Murder at the Chron". The theme, as you can guess, was the goings-on in the offices of the newspaper but with the characters being completely fictitious (in theory). The Chronicle spared no efforts in trying to make the event a succes, even to the extent of printing a fictitious front page to that week's edition of the newspaper. The cast wrote the articles on the front page and hidden in them were clues to the motives of the suspects. The performance duly took place in the marquee on a foul evening on 14th December 2013. At times it seemed as if the marquee was going to blow away! However, we coped and everybody had a good time. What was the mystery charity we were raising funds for and why the secrecy? Well, the charity was the launch of the Prince's Countryside Fund and it coincided with a visit from Prince Charles to the Chronicle's offices, which had to be kept secret for security purposes. And no, we weren't invited to meet the Prince. He was long gone by the time we did the performance. Perhaps it was just as well because I know we had some rabid anti-royalists in the audience. I guess the knighthood had passed me by again!

Les as Callum Inches, Marie-Anne as Paige Free, Rob as Ed Lines, Me as Donald Canard,
Laura as Amy Fiddler, John as Nick Carson and Vikki as Vi Lente.
Sadly Tom had already been murdered when this was taken.

Totally wrapped up in the action, Les, Vikki, Tom, Marilyn and Rob

Above: The cast armed and dangerous. Can't remember how I ended up on the end wearing a fez.
Below: Marie-Anne and Tom Gibson played sister and brother at odds with each other. Being in reality a married couple probably gave them good practice in sounding convincing.

The Golden Gun Awards, yet again (Feb 2014)

This performance was another example of the benefits of keeping the concept simple. We had agreed to perform a murder mystery to raise funds for Llanbedr Village Hall and I was taking my usual role as Don Cortesone, the Godfather and investigator. Two weeks before the show I was admitted to hospital with what turned out to be cellulitis, which as you probably know, is a potentially serious bacterial skin infection. I was being treated with antibiotics but it was uncertain whether I would be discharged in time to play my part in the show. It was decided that we couldn't risk it, so the roles were re-arranged. John Geraghty, who was to play the Irish gunman as he had in a previous performance of this show, took over my role as Don Cortesone, the Godfather, and Rob Tollman, who had also played the victim's son and the gunman in previous shows, stepped in and took on John's role. As luck would have it, I was discharged, albeit with a heavily bandaged arm, on the day of the performance, so I went along as a member of the audience and thoroughly enjoyed it, as did the other members of the audience. The rearranged cast did a superb job. The audience enjoyed it so much that we were immediately asked to perform, and booked for, another murder mystery the following year.

An interesting montage of photographs created by Tom and Marie-Anne (I think)

105

Dai Laughing Productions takes murder on tour for visit to the Isle of Man

DAI Laughing Productions from Abergavenny, which helps to raise funds for good causes by staging murder mystery events, recently headed off on a special mission to the Isle of Man.

The aim was to raise money for the Rob Vine Fund, which was set up to provide medical/rescue equipment and training for all doctors, paramedics and marshals involved in motorsport events on the island.

Writer and producer Don Balkwill explained why the troupe were prepared to undertake a 600-mile round trip to provide just one evening's entertainment free of charge at the Ascot Hotel, Douglas.

"We normally only perform in the South Wales area but towards the end of last year I had a call from the owner of the hotel, who had heard about us through one of his managers, Jon Smith, who hails from Abergavenny.

"They were looking to promote the visibility of the hotel's restaurant, Mackey's, and at the same time raise funds

for the charity.

"After some discussion we agreed to make the trip because we enjoy what we do. It was a bit of an adventure and most of our performers had never visited the Isle of Man before so it was an opportunity not to be missed."

The group decided to perform one of its favourite murder mysteries - 'The Golden Gun Awards for Hitman of the Year 1920'.

It centres on a gangsters and molls get-together, where a Golden Gun is presented to the Best Hitman of the Year.

Unfortunately the hitman of the year gets bumped off before he can receive his award and Don Cortisoni, the leader of the gangsters, carries out an investigation to establish who the murderer is.

"The audience were invited to come dressed as 1920s gangsters and molls, and most of them did," said Don. " It really was a fun evening with plenty to eat and drink, plenty of audience participation and lots of laughter.

"However at the end of the evening disaster struck. Before the guilty party is revealed the audience have to choose who they think carried out the murder - and, unfortunately, no team picked the right person!

"In 20 years of performing murder mysteries this had never happened before. We had to give the answer sheets back so they could try again.

"Luckily this time one team named the murderer, their reason for picking him - 'There was nobody else left!!' Brilliant. Time to relax, have a glass of wine, and enjoy the plaudits. Thankfully everybody, and particularly the hotel's owner, who had taken the risk of shipping us over, was happy with the evening."

BOROUGH THEATRE
ABERGAVENNY

Friday 14 March 8pm
Budapest Gypsy Orchestra
World-class violinist Tcha Limberger is joined by his Gypsy band
£15 (concessions £13)

Saturday 15 March 7.30pm
Brandenburg Bach Soloists
with David Wright, Harpsichord and Fiona Slominaka, Flute
An evening of Handel, Vivaldi and Bach
£16 (concessions £14)

Friday 21 March 6.30pm
Grandpa's Railway
All aboard! A wonderful family show featuring a model railway on stage
£6.50 Family Ticket £24

MORE EVENTS NOW ON SALE!
An Evening with Iolo Williams; AAODS High Society; An Evening with Elvis; Counterfeit 60's Tribute; London Classic Theatre: Entertaining Mr Sloane; Catrin Finch & Seckou Keita; Sounds of Simon (Tribute to Simon & Garfunkel); plus drama, dance, comedy, music, children's shows and more!

Box Office 01873 850805
www.boroughtheatreabergavenny.co.uk
BOOK YOUR TICKETS ONLINE!

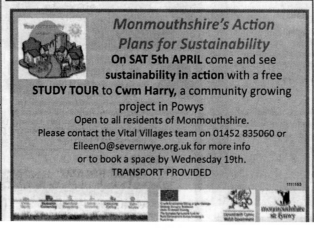

Monmouthshire's Action Plans for Sustainability
On SAT 5th APRIL come and see **sustainability in action** with a free **STUDY TOUR** to **Cwm Harry**, a community growing project in Powys
Open to all residents of Monmouthshire.
Please contact the Vital Villages team on 01452 835060 or EileenO@severnwye.org.uk for more info
or to book a space by Wednesday 19th.
TRANSPORT PROVIDED

Dai Laughing goes on the road (and the sea) March 2014.

Marilyn's son, Jonny, had gone to the Isle of Man to learn about the hotel trade for six months after he left University. Twelve years later he was still there. By this time he was a duty manager with the Ascot Hotel. The hotel owner, Norman Mackey, was looking for ways of promoting their restaurant and Jonny mentioned that his stepfather (me) organised murder mystery events to raise funds for good causes. In no time at all Norman booked us to put on a show in the Hotel with any excess funds going to an IOM charity. Norman agreed to cover all the costs of taking eight people to the island and putting them up at the hotel. After discussion with Norman, it was decided to put on the Golden Gun Awards again, because it is great fun to perform, the audience always enjoy it, and they can all dress up as gangsters or molls. Luckily all the cast, with the exception of John Geraghty who had to work, were available to take part and as I was well again I went back to playing the Godfather. We set off early in the morning on Friday 28th February and drove up to Heysham in Lancashire to catch the afternoon ferry to the Isle of Man. It took nearly four hours to reach the island on the ferry. We were treated royally at the hotel and could eat and drink whatever we wanted. The show was performed on the next night and went exceedingly well although there were a couple of people in the audience who got too involved and kept interrupting the proceedings and were very rude. When Mari-Anne was asked about her memorable moment from the show she said the main one for her, was me putting a mouthy Irishman in his place by telling him that he had to stand up if he wanted to ask a question. It turns out he was already standing up! He wasn't too much trouble after that. (I didn't realise I could be so cruel).

Another amusing moment was when Mark, Vikki's boyfriend, was named as the murderer by one team. Mark had come along with us as a car driver, he hadn't been part of the murder mystery but had sat on his own at a table near to us pretending to be Don Cortesone's bodyguard.

We travelled back on the Sunday morning ferry. On the drive down from Heysham, we had to divert to Liverpool airport to pick up Marilyn who had flown back. As she said, "No way am I going on a ferry across the Irish sea in March". Can't say I blame her because a few of our performers really suffered on the return ferry journey!

However, in spite of that, the whole trip was a great success and Norman wanted us to return the following year and although initial arrangements were made for this to happen it never did because the number of bookings for the evening didn't justify the cost of us all going over.

Norman and I enjoying a glass or two together after the show was over. Entertaining the sponsor is a tough job but somebody has to do it!

107

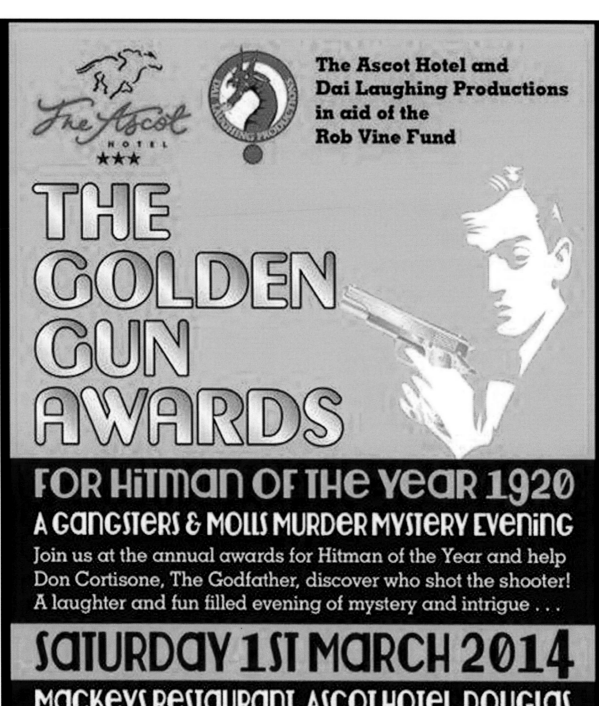

Note the price of the tickets, £49.00 per person. Amazing when you think that the usual charge per person is about £15.00 including the meal.

Mark, at the far end, sat on his own and never said a word yet he was named as the murderer by one section of the audience. He wasn't even in the show!

Look you lot it's always the Godfather who's in charge and that's me!

Our three newbies, Simon, Jaycee and Fiona give 'expression' to their feelings.

It's Murder in Business (May 2014)

It's not often we are asked to perform a show during the day, thank goodness, because getting a cast together on a workday and in the afternoon is a devil of a job. However, this is what Newport Business Club needed, because it's a club for business people who meet during working hours to network and discover what's happening in their area. For example, what the council are dreaming up to make their businesses operate more efficiently (sic). For this show we had to bring in three new faces, Jaycee Withey, Fiona Angwin and Simon Griffiths. Thankfully all three had appeared on stage previously, albeit not in murder mysteries but, they all coped admirably. In addition, because of the difficulty in finding men for that afternoon, I had to write the show using Mari-Anne as the investigator and put myself in as one of the suspects. We also used a member of the club, Stephanie Asabord, as the murder victim. The audience was a bit stiff and formal to begin with, which didn't help poor Mari-Anne on her first time controlling everything. However, she coped well, but as Jaycee put it: "The extreme lack of audience participation was was like pulling teeth and should have put me off for life." Thankfully it didn't and she went on to appear in a number of other shows with us, as did Fiona and Simon. Later that evening I had a call from Janine, who had organised the event and she spent at least twenty minutes singing our praises and saying how much the audience enjoyed the afternoon. According to Janine the reason the audience didn't seem to be involved was that the Business Club people are very competitive so didn't want to ask revealing questions because the other teams might have followed their line of reasoning in finding the murderer. Not that this approach helped anybody, because no team picked the correct suspect at the first time of asking and they all had to try again! The charity which benefited from the performance was 'The Olive Branch' which is a small Newport charity that helps the homeless.

L to R. Marie-Anne Gibson, Les Hayes, Stephanie Asabord, Fiona Angwin, Simon Griffiths, Margaret Barrell, m e and Jaycee Withey.

Has nobody ever taught Fiona and Laura that it's rude to shout at the audience?

John tries to convince the audience that it wasn't him that did the dirty deed. Les responds by pointing out the pig flying past the window.

Rob looks to the heavens for inspiration to prove his innocence whilst Vikki thinks he is going down to hell for telling lies.

Murder To a Tee (two) (June 2014)

Being asked to put on a show for Monmouthshire Golf Club members on Saturday 15th June 2014, gave us the chance to re-use the script written for The NSPCC at West Mon Golf Club from the previous year. This show illustrates how we try, not only to tailor the show to the organisation or the venue but also how we try to use appropriate names for the characters. Hence the newly elected Chairman of 'Swingers Golf Club' was called 'Chip Hookshot' who was a thoroughly bad egg, always hatching plots, and on this occasion, he had laid one too many, because he became the murder victim. The suspects consisted of Albert Ross, a retired forensic scientist. Dr Madeline Caddy who liked to play a round, in more ways than one. Then there was Glen Green the groundsman, a bogey man who believed the answer lay in the soil. Rob Tollman played that role and came over as a thoroughly bad lot which seemed to incense one of the male members of the audience. Fi Angwin who played Dr Caddy, remembers the person as being totally convinced that their groundsman would never behave inappropriately ... I tried to gently remind him that we were all fictional characters and were not trying to cast aspersions on their groundsman in any way. However, he was so incensed that I'm not sure I convinced him. Sometimes people do take things so seriously! The other suspects were Anna Eagle, secretary for Hookshot's company - had she flashed once too often? Could the guilty party be Duff Shott, a smoking gun when it came to Shooters Golf Club or Sandie Bunker the treasurer and banker - she was good with figures but could she have pulled a number? Finally, we had William (Old Bill) Hogan, the retired investigator, did he really have a clue or was he just incompetent?

L to R Back: Les as Albert, John as Duff, Rob as Glen, Martin as Chip, the murder victim. Front: Me as Old Bill, Fiona as Dr. Caddy, Laura as Anna and Vikki as Sandie.

Pam reveals to John that when there was wine left over from communion it didn't get wasted... but the Vicar did!

John was unimpressed.

Les was not only unimpressed he was also depressed that the Vicar had failings.

Vikki was disgusted that Pam should mention the Vicars drinking problem at such a sad time.

Rob couldn't care less, but Fiona though, Oh goody! More wine for me.

114

Murder on the PCC (July 2014)

There are a number of organisations that use the initials PCC - The Press Complaints Commission, Pembrokeshire County Council, Police Crime Commissioners amongst others. In this murder mystery it stands for Parochial Church Council. We were performing a show to raise funds for the Church Parishes of Tretire and Pencoed, which are situated just inside the county of Herefordshire, near Ross-on-Wye. The plot revolved around the nefarious goings of some of the members of a fictitious Church council. There was embezzlement, adultery and of course, murder, all common stuff on a church council, wouldn't you think? The audience, including a vicar, took it all in good part, realising that it was, of course, all make-believe, or maybe they knew something that we didn't! Bye the bye there was no murder on stage with this show, it was supposed to have happened before the meeting started, at a PCC meeting, where else?

Above: The cast prepare themselves for the upcoming interrogation.
Below: The audience lubricate their brain cells to find out who killed their Vicar.

If you're wondering what I'm saying it's:
"How dare you suggest that I'm wearing a
mask, I always look like this."

The Curse of the Dragons Eye (Oct 2014)

This event was actually organised at very short notice. John and Jude Bannon asked us to put on a fundraiser for their daughter who worked for Barnardo's. She was going to Uganda on a short term basis to help support a school there. Because a performance of this show was already organised for later in the month, and our costumes and props were ready for that, we decided to do the same one here. The show was 'The Curse of the Dragon's Eye' and it revolved around a group of people who like to dress up and pretend to be Witches and Warlocks. As in all murder mysteries, someone dies in suspicious circumstances. (well you can't have a murder mystery without someone dying, can you?). This was Tom Ball's debut performance but certainly not his last. The show was held in the Monmouthshire Golf Club, where we had performed on a number of occasions. The audience was mostly made up of members of Rotary, who certainly know how to enjoy themselves, and when the audience enjoy themselves, we do too! It was a great night. Some of the participants made a real effort by dressing up and wearing masks, or were they?

Below: Raising a glass to the audience from left to right. Vikki Cartledge, Pam Bush, John Geraghty, Fiona Angwin, Laura Collins, Tom Ball, Margaret Barrell and me.

Above: Treowen House, Monmouthshire.
Below: Margaret Barrell, Tom Ball, Les Hayes, Hidden behind Les, Fiona Angwin, John Geraghty and Pam Bush. The gentleman in the Dracula cape is Tom's friend, Darren

The Curse of the Dragon's Eye (Oct 2014)

I'd written 'The Curse of the Dragon's Eye' years previously for another organisation but unfortunately, the event had not taken place because of lack of ticket sales. So when I was asked to put on a murder mystery in a spooky Gothic mansion, which was supposedly haunted, I was jubilant. This was Treowen House in Monmouthshire. In addition it was to be performed on Halloween night, October 31st 2014. It seemed the ideal time to revive the 'Dragons Eye'. It was to raise funds for Monmouth Citizens Advice Bureau, another worthy cause. The show gave everybody, including the audience, a chance to dress up outrageously in witches and wizards outfits. It also gave me the chance to use a large artificial ruby, which I had bought purposely for that murder mystery and was used to depict the Dragon's eye. I also had the use of a very impressive wizards staff made by a friend, David Lucas, although unfortunately, I had to give it back after the show.

The venue lived up to expectations, and the audience was great. We always seem to enjoy the show so much more when we have to dress up. Even though this was performed two weeks after the other one, we still had to make some changes because some people were unavailable. Les and Marilyn stepped in, M. as the murder victim. Bill Catling, the organiser of the event, said afterwards, "Don, please pass on our great thanks for all the efforts your fine cast put in on Friday evening. I know that everybody at Treowen really enjoyed the evening. But most important we cleared £719 profit on the evening for the Citizens Advice Bureau. We also had great feedback from some of those that attended. Well done to those who took part."

An animal skull and the 'Dragon's Eye'

Reading out some of the audiences conclusions, before revealing who the name of the murderer was one of the highlights of the evening. Often some of the answers were outrageous and very funny.

You will note that Marilyn, who played the murder victim, is in the background and has made a miraculous recovery. That's the power of the Dragons Eye for you!

Laura shows the Mayor, Martin Hickman, a photo-fit of the prime suspect. Who do you think it looks like.

Tom's lips are moving so we know he's lying, and from the expression on Marie-Anne's face so does she.

As Clerk to the Council Snowy could be the only one telling the truth... But I wouldn't count on it.

I didn't know that these days you can get authorisation by phone to carry out an investigation?

All the suspects ponder on whether their dark secrets will be revealed. Of course they will, you can't solve the mystery without them.

Politics is Murder (Jan 2015)

Having performed seven murder mysteries in 2014, we started on another busy year in January 2015, performing 'Politics is Murder'. This was written by Tom Ball, who was by now one of our regular performers; somebody who was becoming an integral part of Dai Laughing and would take over the running of the group when I stepped down. Stephen (Snowy) Clark, a well known participant in local amateur dramatics, made his debut performance with us, and as you would expect was excellent. He too became a regular performer.

This show was to help raise funds for the Mayor of Abergavenny, Martin Hickman's, charities for 2014/15. As the title suggests the theme was politics. All the suspects were involved in local politics and had dark secrets or were on the fiddle in one way or another. Some might say that this was true to life, however, I couldn't possibly comment! To be fair, the audience, which contained a lot of councillors and local dignitaries, took it all in good part and seemed to thoroughly enjoy themselves. Perhaps these were the honest politicians. Again, I couldn't possibly comment, although, I did wonder why my planning application was rejected so soon after the show! (Just joking). The event was held in the Abergavenny Masons' meeting hall in Abergavenny.

I'm sure you've heard the saying, How can you tell if a politician is lying? Answer: Their lips are moving! And so it was with our suspects. The thing to remember is they were only acting!

L to R. Tom Gibson, Snowy Clark, Marie-Anne Gibson, Laura Collins, Vikki Cartledge, John Geraghty and me.

PAIN

VERNON
CROOK
Treasurer

*As suspects they spend a
lot of time spouting or, as
Margaret is doing, a Tommy
Cooper impression.*

An Optimistic Murder (March 2015)

In March, we did a murder mystery for the Magor 1st & 2nd Brownies, who were supporting Hannah Jones, one of their leaders, who was taking part in the Africa challenge; a four-week expedition to Kenya, in support of the Moving Mountains charity. The show, which we had performed before, was 'An Optimistic Murder'. The theme was the annual dinner of the Newoptimists, a group of people who prefer to look forward rather than back. I wrote this show specifically for the Soroptimist's, but it was easily adapted to any situation. The Chairperson, Cynthia Payne (Pam Bush), is about to make a disclosure that will cause turmoil within the organisation, but someone is out to stop her, permanently! Gill Crandon made her debut in this show, I knew she would be good at telling tall stories because she is an ex-headmistress. It must have been fun because the audience enjoyed themselves tremendously, as we did. Andrea Rodley, commented, "Huge thanks to you all – we had an amazing evening – thank you for your support x". Dib, dib, dib, or is that for cubs only?

Carl Bigmister plies Fay May with wine in the hope that her name lives up to expectations.

You never know when you will need a hand to point you in the right direction of a murder suspect.

123

Featured in a learned Journal (Feb 2015)

Occasionally, I have been contacted by people asking to use extracts from my books or even asking where can they still obtain copies of them, I have to admit, it does make me feel quite proud when this happens. Two occasions stand out in particular. The first was when the National Trust in Plymouth, asked if they could feature pages from The Book of Shaugh Parish in an exhibition which was held in Saltram House, a National Trust property, near Plymouth. The second was being asked by the Chairman of the Plymouth Mineral & Mining Club, Steve Roberts if they could use extracts of the book in their quarterly journal. It covered two A4 pages. Chuffed to bits! Am I being boastful and pretentious? Yes, of course, I am but that's me.

Shaugh Bridge China Clay Dry and Jeffery Jones
From notes extracted by Steve Roberts
from Don Balkwill's Book
'The Book of Shaugh Parish – It's a Shaugh Thing'

As summer 2014 drew to a close and on the day when the country was once again thrust back into the evening gloom of Greenwich Mean Time, I found myself faced with the task of showing a group of our members around the industrial archaeological remains of Shaugh Bridge. Having lived in the village for some six years, I had explored the area fairly thoroughly and so was familiar with many of the remains such as the granite quarries, ferro-ceramic works, iron mine, corn mill, Bickleigh Vale Phoenix copper mine, etc.. The club had visited the site on at least two previous occasions, with members parking on the rough ground in front of the dismantled pan kiln by the bridge. Despite the kiln having been the last of the IA items to have been working, surprisingly little information about it had been forthcoming, save for the basic facts that it had been built in 1888 to serve Watts, Blake and Bearne's Wigford Down pit and that china clay had been transported from the pit to the dry in suspension via a pipeline of a combination of glazed terracotta and cast iron over a mile and three quarters in length.

In my time in the village in the 1980s, I had encountered two men who had worked at the dry and various people who could remember it working, yet none had anything special to say about it, as at the time such structures were merely a place of work and not uncommon. Thus, I was delighted when Don Balkwill's publication "The Book of Shaugh Parish – It's a Shaugh Thing" appeared in 2008. The appearance of the book was no surprise as other family members, friends and I had been contacted by Don and invited to contribute information, yet what was a surprise was a fascinating chapter dealing with the history of the dry and of the family that lived in a cottage that adjoined its furnace end. I know of no other pan kilns like this, though I haven't gone looking for any, and will be quite prepared to hear from any of our members with a special interest in the Cornish Alps, who may have encountered something similar. Of course, it's a well-known fact that Devonshire china clay is superior to that produced in the Duchy, so to find that our Devonshire pan kiln/cottage is unique would be the icing on the cake!

Naturally, I drew heavily on the information in Don's book for the club trip and received various comments to the effect that the information would be of interest to other members via the Journal. I contacted Don, now a resident of Abergavenny, though he grew up in Shaugh, and without hesitation he granted permission for me to 'lift' information from the book for these pages. I do not reproduce it verbatim or in quite the same order, as some aspects are understandably more

Shaugh clay dries c 1920/30

concerned with general social history than with the history that relates directly to the inhabitants of the cottage, but I hope that I have retained the flavour of Don's writing and Jeffery Jones' notes. Sadly, the dry is now badly overgrown, with much detail obscured, and another major clearance of vegetation is required, as last happened seven or eight years ago.

Background - The Jeffery History.

Fred and Annie outside the cottage in 1936

Frederick Jeffery married Mary Ann (Annie) Ash in 1900 at St Jude's church in Plymouth. By 1901, they were living at Shaugh Bridge. Frederick was 27 and worked as a clay miner. They lived in the small cottage attached to the clay dry. The cottage and kiln were built in 1888. There was a front room, a kitchen/dining room in the back and two bedrooms upstairs. The back wall of the cottage was built into the side of the rock face. Frederick and Annie had six children in twelve years – three boys and three girls. Sadly, one of the boys (William) died in a tragic accident at the nearby mill in 1915. Frederick was a handyman/carpenter and had the 'first running toilet' in the area.

One of their children, Hilda, married Frank Jones in 1929 and their son Jeffery Edward Jones was born in 1935 in Exeter but was raised by his grandparents in the cottage at Shaugh kiln. According to Jeffery's daughters this was because his mother 'became ill during his birth'.

Notes from Jeffery Edward Jones

My earliest memories centre around the tiny stone-built cottage, built as part of a china clay works drying kiln which was constructed in 1888 at Shaugh Bridge. We were there because my granddad, a real jack of all trades (carpenter, blacksmith, haircutter, cobbler and saw sharpener) had worked as a maintenance man for the clay company. He and Gran were married in 1900 and I believe moved straight into the cottage – they certainly had their six children in it. Quite an achievement considering it had precisely two small upstairs rooms and two slightly larger ones downstairs – no running water, walls that oozed dampness, little light and must have been as unhealthy as one could get. I don't recall it ever getting hot, although there was a total lack of fresh air – particularly in the back bedroom 1 – a long, narrow room with a tiny window at one end. The cottage was built into the clayworks in such a way that the back and one side were completely blanked off – the back wall was, in effect, the vertical rockface of the bank, while the side wall was the end wall of the drying kiln shed. We also had a small workers' eating place (filthy with coal dust from the [furnace] room) immediately above the back bedroom.

It seemed normal – probably because as a child I was so isolated that I saw the insides of very few other houses, all primitive, but some fairly large farms and other tiny cottages – all stone built.

An Optimistic Murder again (April 2015)

Although this show had the same name as the one we performed the previous month, the fact is that no two shows are ever the same. For a start, we had three different cast members, Jaycee Withey, Snowy Clark and Tom Ball. Changing the cast always alters the dynamics of any performance. What with that, and a totally different audience, you would hardly recognise it as being the same show. In addition, all the suspects have a motive to commit the murder so, you could have a different ending every time, if you wanted to. (We did love to confuse people).

This performance was for the Abergavenny Soroptimist's, and it was performed in Llanfoist Village Hall. They were raising funds for the Endometriosis charity, Endometriosis, is a particularly nasty gynaecological disease which affects quite a few women, but is rarely talked about, and so it is not well understood. The show was a hit helping to raise over £1,000, and as one of the audience, Helen Gee, commented the show was "Spectacular". Well, with suspects like Juan Latiff, Vernon Crook, Carl Bigamister, Fay May, Cynthia Pain, Dr Harriet Shipman, Luce Moralis and retired policeman Richard (Don't call me Dick) Head investigating, I suppose it had to be.

Pam Bush, me, Jaycee Withey, Snowy Clark, Margaret Barrell, Tom Ball, Gill Crandon, and John Geraghty

Former mayoress accepts cheque

FORMER Abergavenny mayoress Alison Hickman has received a cheque for £1,000 from Abergavenny Soroptimists on behalf of Endometriosis UK.

The group raised the money by hosting a successful murder mystery evening organised by local company Dai Laughing Productions.

Speaking at the presentation, Mrs Hickman explained that one in ten women in the UK suffer from the painful gynaecological condition with more that 176 sufferers worldwide.

On average it takes more than seven years to diagnose the condition and as yet there it no definite cure.

• Alison Hickman accepting a cheque from Ann Payne

A view of this beautiful little church from towards the back. There were other tables behind the photographer and as you can just see there were tables to the left. Because of the layout of the church some of the audience had their view partially obscured by pillars and archways. Unfortunately, the powers that be wouldn't let us remove them!

Janine Davies as Theresa Green came over as a very sincere and honest person: just shows how looks can be deceptive! She is a good actress.

Perhaps if I'd had an Irish accent and was called Paisley maybe my life would have been completely different. Starting a speech with "Right m'dears this is what I want you to do Oh arr" doesn't quite command the same respect. Ah well! at least I got to direct proceedings from the pulpit.

Murder on the PCC (June 2015)

You may remember that we performed this show in July of 2014. I'd told my friends Verley and Les Toyah about it, and they, being on the PCC for St Teilo's Church, were interested in having the show performed for them because they are also members of a group called HOST which organises events and such like to raise funds for the church. It was enormous fun, and for me, one of the most memorable and enjoyable performances of my murder mystery career. As with the last murder mystery we did for St Teilo's, we performed in the church again. I was there in my usual role of investigator, but this time I was able to conduct the whole thing from the pulpit. I never realised before that standing in a pulpit can give you such a feeling of power. I took full advantage of my position at the lectern to order everybody around but the audience didn't seem to mind a bit. I bet you are thinking I'm power crazy and perhaps I am. My wife, Marilyn, complains that I'm always telling her what to do. It's not true of course It's just that sometimes people need to be pointed in the right direction!

Janine Davies performed her first, of many roles for Dai Laughing and was excellent.

This is what Verley had to say the following day: "Hi Don, am so happy to confirm that 'Murder on the PCC' was a huge success. Thanks to Dai Laughing, we made a very healthy profit of £600.00 for St. Teilo's funds. Please tell your friends that we cannot praise or thank them enough. The new vicar, Fr. Julian Gray, was particularly impressed by the generosity of your group in both the gifts of their time and talents." These sort of comments made the time and effort spent all worthwhile.

Vikki Carteledge as Clarisa Bell, John Geraghty as Ivor Coffin, Janine Davies as Theresa Green, Laura Collins as Angelina Heaven, Snowy Clark as Christian Bishop, me as Robin Graves and Tom Ball as St John Church. No, Tom's not asleep just resting his eyelids!

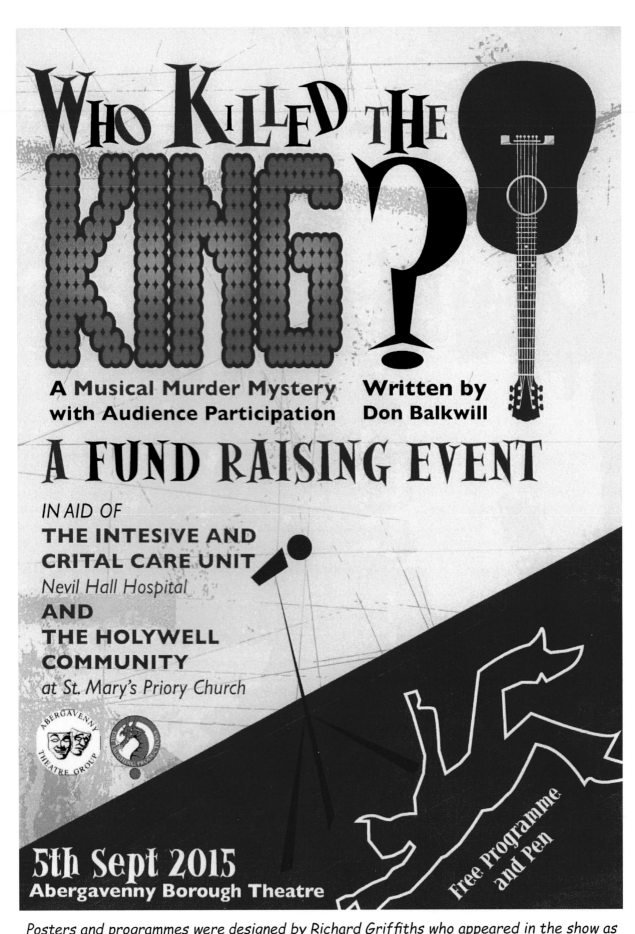

Posters and programmes were designed by Richard Griffiths who appeared in the show as part of the Blues Brothers tribute act, well, you have to support local businesses don't you?

Who Killed the King? (Sept 2015)

During 2014, I had started thinking about killing off my involvement with the murder mystery shows. (See the play on words even at this late stage). Firstly, because even with all the pleasure they had given me I was getting tired of writing, organising and appearing in them; after all it had been 20 years since my first murder mystery. Secondly, I wanted to concentrate on writing another book, and finally because I wanted to develop my public speaking role with local groups and organisations. The latter two reasons were related to the weekly newspaper articles on gadgets that I had been writing since 2011. Having said all that, I wanted to finish my involvement with Dai Laughing Productions with a bang. I wanted to do a show that raised more money for a good cause than any other event we had performed before, and that was why "Who killed the King" was conceived. We usually performed in front of audiences of up to about 60, so to raise a lot more money we had to have a much larger audience. So I decided that I would try and put on a show in the Abergavenny Borough Theatre. I knew it would cost a lot to hire the venue, but I also knew it would hold more people. To bring in a large audience it made sense to have a well-known name in the cast that would draw in the crowds. Luckily, in Abergavenny, we have a very popular Elvis Presley impersonator called Keith Davies, who has raised many hundreds of thousands of pounds for good causes. As luck would have it, Keith was a supporter of Dai Laughing and had attended a number of our shows, so we had got to know him quite well. I suggested to Keith that I write a show around him, where he sang a few songs but to save him having to do any acting we then use him as the murder victim. Luckily, Keith agreed, and I set about writing the show. I decided to write it as a musical murder mystery, something that I had never done before. The plot revolved around seven tribute acts, led by Elvis, who are performing on stage when Elvis gets bumped off. A retired policeman then takes over and the investigation takes place. Whilst writing the script I had envisaged the death scene would be that Elvis, after singing his first song, would pick a guitar, plug it in, and would be electrocuted. Boom! After discussions with Keith this was changed because it was felt that there may be people who would associate the electrocution with Keith's real life occupation as MD of a well respected electrical business in Abergavenny. We couldn't have that could we?, So I changed the scene. We still had the electrical explosion, all the theatre lights went out and when they came on again Elvis was collapsed on the floor. But! Elvis hadn't been electrocuted he had been poisoned so it was Aargh!!! not Boom!

We tried lots of different ways to kill off Keith but he he still kept on singing. It was the poison that got him in the end, but even then he came back from the dead!

Who Killed the King

Most of the members of Dai Laughing, were also members of Abergavenny Theatre Group, which in turn is part of the A4B group (Acting4TheBorough), a voluntary organisation made up of amateur theatrical groups who use the Borough Theatre in Abergavenny. The group is dedicated to promoting and supporting the theatre's amateur community. One of the benefits of being a member of the group is that they get preferential rates when hiring the theatre. In an effort to maximise the return from the performance, I suggested that Dai Laughing and ATG put on the show as a joint venture. To be honest, when I first floated the idea to the members of DL and ATG, I think it fair to say that there was some scepticism as to whether a murder mystery could work in a theatre, or whether enough customers would come to the show to cover the costs. However, I had no doubts, as I had done something similar before, and I knew Keith would be a big draw in helping to bring in an audience. I was so convinced, that I said, I would personally cover any loses if the show failed. On that basis, the joint undertaking was agreed. There followed many months of writing and adapting the script, holding auditions to find singers, approaching local businesses and organisations to provide sponsorship, and of course many hours of rehearsals.

The Chosen Tribute Acts L. to R. Tom Ball (Don McLean), Rob Tollman (Meatloaf), Jaycee Withey (Tina Turner), Mari-Anne Gibson (Britney Spears), Emma-Jayne Morris (Cher) Me (I can't sing), John Geraghty (Dr Crippen - not a tribute), Inset; Keith Davies (Elvis Presley), Richard Griffiths (Elwood Blues) and Matt Lane (Jake Blues)

Who Killed the King?

The tickets were priced fairly high for an amateur production at £15.00 per head, perhaps in retrospect a little too high. However, I felt that the audience would be happy to pay that when they knew that the majority of the proceeds were going to the Intensive and Critical care unit in our local hospital, Nevill Hall, with the balance going to The Holywell Community at St Mary's Priory Church. The evening of the show arrived, and we had an audience of over 200 people, despite a large party not being able to attend. Everything went smoothly, and the show was a roaring success. All the performers were excellent and thoroughly deserved the standing ovation they got at the end. But it wasn't only the singers/actors we shouldn't forget our dancers, Georgia Withey and Megan Guy. Then there were the minor roles that were so essential, John Geraghty, who played two small roles and stage managed as well, people like Bryan Green and Mike Dennington from the Memphis Mafia who struggled to carry the body off stage and through the auditorium doors. We never expected the audience to become so involved so there were dozens of questions. Fiona Angwin had the difficult task of sorting the relevant questions before handing them to me. Then there were all the helpers who collected the questions from the audience, Hilary Geraghty, Tom Gibson, Clive Davies, Jennie Tagg, and Marilyn, my wife, Everybody worked hard to make the show a success and it was!

The opening scene; Elvis (Keith) leads the other tribute acts onto the stage and starts the show by singing that rousing song 'See See Rider' and then follows up with 'Devil in Disguise' whilst the others sit and wait for their slot.
Note: Matt as Jake Blues is on stage but out of shot.

The Story

An Elvis Presley sound-alike, Kevin Carter, heads a troupe of tribute acts who perform throughout South Wales. They earn a limited amount of income by performing at functions and in venues like Hotels or Theatres.

All monies received are put into a bank account from which expenses are paid, monies left over at the end of the financial year are shared out, with 25% going to Kevin and the balance shared equally amongst the other acts. Like the majority of tribute acts this does not pay sufficiently well for the performers to be able to give up their day jobs.

Although on the face of it they appear to be a happy band they all secretly harbour the desire to front the troupe. Besides this there are seething resentments towards Kevin for the way he treats them. One performer, or is it two, feels so aggrieved that they decide remove Kevin permanently......

'YOUR' part in the Investigation

As you arrive you were given this programme and slips of paper. The programme tells you who is who, the slips of paper are for you to write down your teams questions, and the answer sheet is for you to write down who you think did it. Write down your questions as you think of them. Periodically there will be short breaks in the proceedings for them to be collected.

Please don't leave your seats during these breaks, just pass your questions down to the end of the rows. There will be a 20 minute break at approximately 8.30 for you to have an ice-cream or a drink if you wish.

Your questions must be directed to an individual and not to the group as a whole. One thing to remember is this, only the murder or murderers will lie, the others may bend the truth but if asked a direct question they must tell the truth. During the last break your solution will be collected and judged before the murderer(s) is revealed.

Don't forget to boo and hiss the baddies. **Happy Sleuthing.**

The players in order of Appearance

The Announcer, *Doesn't actually appear but he is there* .... **John Geraghty**

Jack Green as Jake Blues, *Blues Brothers tribute* .... **Matt Lane**

Dick Green as Elwood Blues, *Blues Brothers Tribute* .... **Richard Griffiths**

Susi Stiles as Britney Spears .... **Mari-Anne Gibson**

Beefy Balls as Meatloaf .... **Rob Tollman**

Gemma Laine as Cher .... **Emma-Jayne Morris**

Ron Colgate as Don McLean .... **Tom Ball**

Kasey Klein as Tina Turner .... **Jaycee Withey**

Kevin Carter as Elvis Presley .... **Keith Davies**

Noah Clewes Semi retired ex-Policeman .... **Don Balkwill**

Dr. Crippen the Doctor on hand and Pathologist .... **John Geraghty**

Other Characters:

Burke & Hare, Stretcher Bearers .... **Bryan Green & Mike Dennington**

Ina Vestigate, Noah Clewes assistant .... **Fiona Angwin**

The Dancers, Kover Girls .... **Georgia Withey & Megan Guy**

Meet the Cast

Jaycee Withey (as Tina Turner) has travelled all over South Wales and parts of North and West England, for 20 years as a professional singer of cabaret, pop and rock songs She manages this career besides looking after the family home and their three children!

Keith Davies (as Elvis Presley) probably better known as the "Abergavenny Elvis" has over the last ten years helped to raise over £275,000 for good causes. All this besides running his business, Abergavenny Electrics, and being president of Abergavenny Rotary.

Don Balkwill (as Noah Clewes) is the writer and director of this show and is a founding member of Dai laughing Productions but has been writing and appearing in Murder Mystery fund raising events for over 20 years. (This show is probably his Swan Song.)

Fiona Angwin (as Ina Vestigate) loves amateur theatre and is a member of both Dai Laughing and ATG. She works professionally as a storyteller and puppeteer (The Yarn Spinner), actress, writer, director, producer, lyricist, set designer, prop-maker and zoologist!

Georgia Withey (Kover Girls dancer) aged only thirteen has been a performer in numerous productions with Stagecoach Theatre Arts since the age of four. She also took a lead role in the short film" Raine River" which premiered at the Cannes Film Festival in 2013.

Megan Guy (Kover Girls dancer) is aged seventeen and is also a member of Stagecoach Theatre Arts having appeared in a number of their shows the latest of which was as "Fantine" in Les Miserables.

Bryan Green & Mike Dennington (Burke & Hare, stretcher bearers) better known as part of the Memphis Mafia, they regularly appear with Keith Davies.

Meet the Cast

John Geraghty (as Dr Crippen and the Announcer) is one of the best known and talented faces in Abergavenny amateur theatre being involved in numerous plays over the years both onstage and backstage. He is also an accomplished linguist who is fluent in more than nine languages.

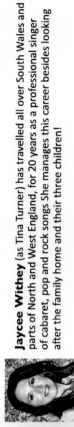

Matt Lane (as Jake Blues) who often performs as part of a tribute act for the Brothers of Blues is also a self employed plumber and a professional DJ operating all over South Wales.

Richard Griffiths (as Elwood Blues) the other half of the tribute act for the Blues Brothers. Also sings with that well known close-harmony male voice choir, "Synergy" and Tenovus Cancer Charity Choir, besides being a talented graphic designer with his own business, I-Deal Designs.

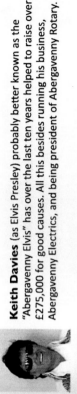

Mari-Anne Gibson (as Britney Spears) started singing at the age of 14 in her local church band. She is also a talented actress and has appeared in a number of productions for Abergavenny Theatre Group and Dai Laughing Productions.

Rob Tollman (as Meatloaf) not only performs with Abergavenny Theatre Group and Dai Laughing Productions but has the distinction of having appeared at the Edinburgh Festival in 2009 with Abergavenny Sidelights Society. He also likes to perform in drag.

Emma-Jayne Morris (as Cher) has been singing for 25 years and is a vocal coach for Mayzmusik Performing Arts Academy. She is also the director and founder of VIG Theatre Company besides being a performer with Abergavenny Theatre Group.

Tom Ball (as Don McLean), a singer and performer in bands since the age of 14, touring the USA twice in a Blues band from Chicago. He has also appeared in numerous local plays and pantomimes. He now performs with, and writes scripts for, Dai Laughing Productions.

133

Elvis has a drink, picks up his guitar and the lights go out. When they come on again Elvis is lying on the floor and I, as his ex-policeman minder, Noah Clewes, have taken charge. (I would have shown you the photo of the blackout scene but you couldn't see a thing). I ask if there is a doctor in the house and Dr. Crippen (John Geraghty) makes his appearance and declares he is dead.

Whilst waiting to find out how Elvis died from 'Autopsies-R-Us' we decide that the show must go on so, the Blues Brothers (Richard and Matt) got the audience going with their rousing rendition of 'Soul Man'.

Tom, performing as Don McLean, did such an excellent acoustic rendition of 'American pie' that the audience couldn't help but join in.

Jaycee's tribute to Tina Turner singing 'Proud Mary' nearly brought the house down, not to be outdone Rob did a powerful rendition of Meatloaf's 'I'd do anything for Love' that certainly stirred the audience.

Mari-Anne belted out her Britney Spears tribute accompanied by the 'Kover Girls' Georgia and Megan.

Apologies for the quality of some of the photographs but they were taken from upstairs in the balcony at the rear of the theatre

Emma- Jayne provided the perfect ending for the tributes songs with her stunning rendition of Cher's 'Walking in Memphis'

Guess who was drinking Red Bull throughout the show? But it was for a good reason, it was so the dead Elvis soundalike could make his return to the stage.
Well they do say it gives you wings!

Appropriately enough he then sang that well known Elvis song 'Angel'

For the Finale Keith led the whole cast in singing that Elvis classic 'Can't help falling in Love' He then told the audience that I was going to give a rendition about a big bird, 'Swan Song' I think it was called. Didn't he know I can't sing!

With ticket sales and donations we grossed over £3,300.00. but more of that later. When it was all over my primary emotion was one of joy and relief at the success of the show however, I also felt vindicated that this type of format can and did work.

Thanks to Tom Gibson who took the photographs

Happy Birthday to 'The Don'

Surprise 70th Birthday Party (14 Sept 2015)

About a week after we had performed 'Who Killed the King' it was my 70th birthday. Marilyn was taking me out to one of my favourite eating places, the Brasserie Italian Restaurant in Abergavenny. When we arrived, imagine my surprise to find a group of people from Dai Laughing and Abergavenny Theatre Group were there already to celebrate with me. They had clubbed together to organise the surprise for me. The meal was, as usual, excellent and even more so because I was sharing it with a group of friends (not the meal but the experience). I was also presented with a Cluedo apron, which I thought was very apt, and a lovely card which the group had gone to a lot of trouble to put together using photographs of me from previous shows. I felt very proud but also humbled that they had gone to all that trouble.

L. to R.
Les Hayes, Marilyn, Tony Tagg (unusually for him enjoying a glass of wine), Gill Crandon and Jenny Tagg

L. to R.
Andrew Williams (enjoying his pot plant), Les Hayes and Marilyn

L. to R.
Martin Crandon (looking very sombre), Mark Samuel, Rob Tollman, Jaycee Withey and a bemused looking git on the end!

To paraphrase an old advert; The best Fish and Chips in the World, probably!
I can attest they are delicous! Page's, Cwmbran.

The suspects L. to R. Tom Gibson, Snowy Clark, Janine Davies in colourful wellies, Margaret
Barrell, me hidden by Tom Ball, and Marilyn.

The audience was very involved and enthusiastic, so much so that they gave a us a standing
ovation at the end of the evening.

What a Fracking Murder (Oct 2015)

Back in April 2014, we had performed a murder mystery in a Fish and Chip Restaurant in Cwmbran, on behalf of Friends of the Earth Torfaen. The theme was the AGM of the Benevolent Soil Society, an eco-friendly group trying to save the planet by planting trees. The only trouble was that one of the committee members was bent on putting the Chairperson into the ground instead. Perhaps the answer does lie in the soil! Unfortunately, as far as I'm aware no photographs were taken on that night and so it does not appear in this album. However, the organisers were so pleased with the results that they asked us to do another one using the same venue. Pam Bush, a long time performer with Dai Laughing, wanted to have a go at writing a murder mystery so we collaborated on this show. We finished up with another successful evening for Friends of the Earth, performing 'What a Fracking Murder', which as you can guess had the topical theme of fracking. Tom Ball took over the role of the investigator and Margaret Barrell's husband Richard, stepped in at the last minute as the murder victim. All went well and the fish and chips supper was delicious! (We don't do these shows just for the free meals, honest!).

There's something you don't often see; a happy bunch of protesters!
Pam Bush and Tom Ball holding the placards and Richard Barrell the murder
victim sitting down

The hall was stunning, we thought fame at last, all this for our benefit, then we realised that Christmas was only a few weeks away.

Old friends Joan Paines, Carolyn Gully and Pam Allinson, with whom I had started performing with over 20 years previously (in the nicest possible way of course).
Old work colleague Noel Jenkinson with white moustache is sitting at the table behind.

Opera is Murder (Nov 2015)

Pam Allinson and I had collaborated on a number of projects over the years. We had both appeared in our very first murder mystery show back in 1994. We had written two of the pantomimes performed for Cascade and we had collaborated on the two murder mysteries that were performed for Barry Soroptimist's, so we stayed in touch over the years. Pam, who was involved not only with the Soroptimist's but with numerous cancer charities besides, got in touch again in early 2015 and asked us to put on a murder mystery for 'Cardiff and Vale Breast Cancer Now' group in Barry. Tom Ball, who was by now taking over the running of Dai Laughing, wrote 'Opera is Murder' The reason for the opera theme was because a professional opera singer, who supported the breast cancer charity had agreed to be the murder victim. On a dank winter's night at the end of November, we drove over 40 miles and eventually found the venue and the show got underway. It was another success. What made it particularly pleasurable for me was that three old friends, not only Pam but also Joan and Carolyn, who had appeared in shows with me years ago, were there and we were able to have a good catch up. On top of that, after the performance, I was approached by Noel Jenkinson, someone who I had worked with over 40 years ago. He had recognised the name on the programme and of course me (I'm sure I haven't changed physically in all that time.) I'm sorry Noel that I didn't recognise you straight away. Well, I am over 70!

Above L. to R. Romin Hanz, Libby Retto, Mike Stand, Dee Varr, Phyllis Steyn, Dor Handel, Bella Cante and Evan Elpus.
Below: The Diva, Phyllis Steyn, gives her speech unaware that it is her last!

143

L. to R. Father Mark Soady, two youngsters from the Holywell community, Mari-Anne Gibson, Keith Davies, me, Richard Griffiths and John Geraghty.

Presenting the cheque for Nevill Hall Intensive and Critical care unit to Senior Nurse Manager Sally Copner.

Presentation of cheques - WKTK (Dec 2015)

At last, we were able to hand over the proceeds from 'Who Killed the King?' performed on 5th September 2015. There was a net total of £2,633.25 raised after expenses, of which £1,974.93 went to Nevill Hall Intensive and Critical Care Unit and £658.32 to The Holywell Community based at St Mary's Church. You may wonder why it took so long before handing over the money. Although in the heat of the moment people offer donations and sponsorship, all in good faith, when it comes to actually handing over the money, well, that can sometimes be a bit problematical, even the theatre was a bit slow in handing over the proceeds from the ticket sales. But, eventually, after a bit of chasing, we received all that had been promised. Father Mark Soady volunteered the use of the Priory Centre for the presentation of the cheques to both organisations. Father Mark and representatives of the Holywell Community received their cheque and Sally Copner, the Senior Nurse Manager of the Critical Care Unit Nevil Hall, received their cheque.

A spin-off benefit from making the donation to the Critical Care Unit was that I happened to mention to Sally that I was in the process of writing a book, the sales from which I hoped to able to make a donation to the Wales Air Ambulance. Sally told me that one of the consultants in her department was a Dr Ami Jones, who was also a critical care doctor with the Wales Air Ambulance, but more of that later.

Those cheques must have come from from a very big cheque book which I wouldn't want to carry around!

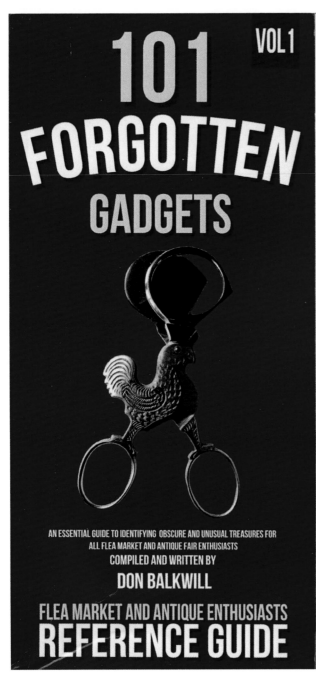

101 FORGOTTEN GADGETS

VOL 1

101 Forgotten Gadgets

Have you ever been to an antique fair or market and found an obscure object but not known the name or purpose of it, this reference guide will be a great addition to help your knowledge and collection grow. These gadgets that have been found and collected over the past couple of years illustrate social history and changing times, ranging from the 1500's up to the 1900's. Some gadgets that even dealers have had trouble identifying, but with the help of collectors, acquaintances and a gadget with advanced technology (the computer), a list of 101 forgotten gadgets has been created for all you enthusiasts.

AN ESSENTIAL GUIDE TO IDENTIFYING OBSCURE AND UNUSUAL TREASURES FOR ALL FLEA MARKET AND ANTIQUE FAIR ENTHUSIASTS

COMPILED AND WRITTEN BY

DON BALKWILL

FLEA MARKET AND ANTIQUE ENTHUSIASTS REFERENCE GUIDE

UK £9.95

Black Sheep Print & Publishing Ltd
The Corn Bin Stanley Rd, Garndiffaith
Pontypool, Torfaen NP4 7LH

www.forgottengadgets.com

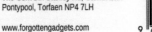

ISBN 978-0-9935467-0-9

9 780993 546709

The front and back covers of the finished book. It had been designed so that it would easily slip into your pocket if you were at a flea market or antiques fair. If you saw something that you didn't recognise or thought was vaguely familiar, the idea was that you would then look it up in this little book. In reality the chances of you seeing something that was featured in the book are pretty slim when you consider the amount of not readily recognisable old objects that are out there. I wrote roughly 350 articles on 'Grandma's Gadgets' for the Chronicle and I had hardly scratched the surface. If you look at the top of the front cover you will see that this is just volume 1. The original plan had been that if this book was successful we would have followed up with volume 2, 3, 4, 5 etc. But, of course that never happened.

I wonder if in years to come somebody will buy a copy of this book, (second hand of course), like it, and then go on the hunt for the follow up volumes?

101 Forgotten Gadgets, (Published 2016)

You may remember that I mentioned earlier that back 2014 I wanted to write another book, This one was to be based on the Grandma's Gadgets articles that I had written for the Abergavenny Chronicle. Well, I had decided that it was going to be a quiz book and although I had made an approach to a publisher in Yorkshire who showed some interest, to be honest I wasn't concerned whether they took it up or not. What I really wanted was to make sure that all the hours of work that I had put into writing the articles didn't go to waste. I wasn't really interested in making money from the book (very few authors make money from reference books anyway) but of course I did want to see my name in print again! (I did say this was a vanity project, didn't I?) Whilst the publishers were thinking about my proposal I decided that if they didn't ahead I would go along the self-publishing route as I done with my first book and as I'm doing with this one.

But, fate was about to take a hand. In July 2015 I had to go to Nevil Hall Hospital for my annual Diabetic Eye Screening, (Diabetes, just another of my ailments.) Anyway, I was sitting in the waiting room and I picked up a copy of 'Living Wales', a free local lifestyle magazine. As I skimmed through it I came across an advert for Black Sheep Publishing, which was based in Garndiffaith near Pontypool. They advertised that besides publishing the magazine I was reading, they also provided graphic and printing services. As they were based not far from Abergavenny I decided to give them a call, to find out how much it would cost to have my book printed with them. This I did the following day. I spoke to the MD, Ben Maassen, and explained what I wanted to do. He invited me down to their offices to discuss it and I duly went along a few days later. I showed him the articles I had already written and copies of my previous two books. The upshot of that meeting was that Ben suggested that instead of just printing the book, they would take over the whole thing and publish and promote the book as well? This meant they would be covering the entire costs. I was cock-a-hoop. As you can imagine we had further discussions about a contract, layout, size, title, and in particular what market we were aiming the book at. Ben thought that we would get better sales if we aimed for the flea market and antique collectors market, so the book should be a reference guide rather than a quiz book. I didn't put up much of an argument against that because he was paying the bills and all I wanted was to see my work published.

Although willing and enthusiastic, Ben and his team had no previous experience of publishing books, so it was a case of us all mucking in to make the project a success. The staff at BSP created a very impressive website together with a blog and Facebook page and as I rewrote the articles they commenced the editing and compilation of the book.

SUPPORT THE WALES AIR AMBULANCE SERVICE

AMBIWLANS AWYR CYMRU
WALES AIR AMBULANCE

Only £9.95 + POSTAGE & HANDLING

VOL1

101 FORGOTTEN GADGETS

AN ESSENTIAL GUIDE TO IDENTIFYING OBSCURE AND UNUSUAL TREASURES FOR ALL FLEA MARKET AND ANTIQUE FAIR ENTHUSIASTS
COMPILED AND WRITTEN BY DON BALKWILL

FLEA MARKET AND ANTIQUE ENTHUSIASTS
REFERENCE GUIDE

PRE ORDER

"101 FORGOTTEN GADGETS" BEFORE 1ST FEBRUARY 2016 AND HELP THE WALES AIR AMBULANCE SERVICE.

101 Forgotten Gadgets - The essential guide to unusual and obscure treasures for all Antique Fair and Flea Market Enthusiasts.

Written and compiled by Don Balkwill from his "Grandma's Gadgets" articles which have appeared in his weekly newspaper column over the last five years.

The book contains 101 photographs and descriptions of gadgets and gizmos not immediately recognisable.

HOW TO ORDER

As I'd already had some experience of publishing with my previous books I was able to make some suggestions that I knew would help to promote it and get advance sales. One of these was to offer people who purchased the book prior to publication the opportunity to have their names, (or names of recipients), printed in the back of the book. As result of this initiative, 200 of the print run of 500 were sold fairly quickly.

You may have gathered from reading this book that I enjoy raising money for good causes so I suggested that we should offer to donate £2.50 to charity for every book preordered and paid for. The chosen charity was the Wales Air Ambulance. I contacted their fundraising department to explain and they agreed that we could use their logo.

Ben had flyers printed up with the details, see above, the order form was on the back. These were to be distributed in the 'Living Wales' magazine, by the Wales Air Ambulance shop in Abergavenny and, by myself.

I also contacting Sally Copner from the Critical Care unit in Nevill Hall Hospital and asked to be put in contact with Dr Ami Jones. I explained to Dr Jones what we were doing and asked if she would endorse this by having a photograph taken holding a flyer, she agreed, so on Thursday 14th January 2016 I set off to Swansea. I was aware of the good work that the Wales Air Ambulance does in providing emergency care for those who face life-threatening illness or injuries, I came back totally convinced that we had chosen the right charity to support. The reason? I met some of the dedicated people who worked at their air ambulance base, which was then situated near Swansea Airport. As you can imagine I felt very honoured and grateful to be welcomed at the base. Tom, Jason, Rhian and Sally gave me a warm welcome and tour. Then Ami landed after being on a call-out and she was also very welcoming and the photographs on the next page were taken.

Dr. Ami Jones with an enlarged copy of the flyer.

In case you are unaware besides being a Consultant and a Flying Doctor, Ami is also a Lieutenant Colonel in the Army Reserves. She has undertaken two tours of duty in Afghanistan. and is also a part of the 'EMRTS Cymru', (Emergency Medical Retrieval and Transfer Service) team, and has been since its inception in 2015. She is a consultant onboard the aircraft as well as being the South Wales Base Lead. In May 2017, she became the interim National Director of the Service and was awarded an MBE as well. During this current Covid-19 Pandemic she has often appeared on television giving updates on critical care. A truly remarkable lady!!

I get in the picture too. Well, if I didn't people might not believe me when I said I went to the Air Ambulance base and met Dr.Ami Jones.

101 Forgotten Gadgets, (Published 2016)

A few days later, on 17th January, I went to the BBC Studios in Cardiff to be interviewed by Roy Noble about my collection of Forgotten Gadgets and my upcoming book. It went very well according to the Studio Director, Charlotte Evans, and I was allowed to chatter on beyond the normal allotted time. In fact, it went so well that I was invited back to do another show in May. One of the spin-off benefits of the radio show was that I was contacted by Mel Jenkins who had been a close friend over 40 years previously, when I had lived in Aberdare. Since that time we have re-kindled our friendship and have met on numerous occasions. We have continued to keep in touch by video call during lockdown. Only trouble is when I see Mel it makes me realise how old I've got!

Roy examines one of the objects I took in which was a Chinese ceramic headrest. These were not only used as a a pillow when sleeping but sometimes found in coffins! Dead uncomfortable I would have thought.

If it could have been proved that it was a genuine antique it would have been worth a fortune as it was I paid only a pound for it. Bargain.

In May I took in a different selection of objects. The one I'm holding is called a marrow spoon. These were used in Victorian times to remove marrow from mainly beef bones. Roast bone marrow was considered to be somewhat of a delicacy in those days but it went out of fashion, although it has made a bit of a comeback in up-market restaurants. Roy said he had tried it but it made him feel sick!
Some recomendation.

101 Forgotten Gadgets, (Published 2016)

In my opinion, one of the most important things to do with any book is to have it distributed to the local libraries. If you can organise for them to be donated instead of them having to be purchased then that's even better. Not only does it benefit cash strapped local libraries but it also creates extra and positive publicity. Back in 2008 Sibelco had agreed to sponsor 'The Book of Shaugh Parish' for distribution to the libraries in Plymouth so I thought it made sense to find a sponsor for this book. I approached William Griffiths of The Angel Hotel in Abergavenny who readily agreed to sponsor 30 copies to be given to the local libraries. When I informed Abergavenny library and told them they were getting copies of the book they organised a presentation and a book launch to be held at the library.

From left to right are Julie Warburton (Abergavenny Library), William Griffiths (The Angel Hotel), Ben Maassen (Black Sheep Publishing), Don Balkwill and Janet Karn (Acting Chief Librarian).

What a brilliant evening superbly organised by Julie and Claire of Abergavenny Library with the approval of Cheryl Haskell, the Community Hub manager. The launch and presentation of the book went very well indeed. The room, which was filled to capacity, saw William Griffiths of the Angel Hotel donate 30 copies of the book ready to be distributed amongst the libraries in the area.

The presentation was followed by my quiz/talk on old gadgets to a very appreciative and knowledgeable audience. All in all the evening was a massive success with a full house, nibbles, drinks and a lot of fun and laughter. I owe a big thank you to everybody involved in the organising and to all those who attended the evening.

These are the sort of gadgets I used in the talk/quiz. How many can you identify?

As a follow on to this event I had an email a few days later from Chepstow Library. It said: "I have been hearing great feedback regarding the launch of your book '101 Forgotten Gadgets' at Abergavenny Library including the 'show and tell' quiz and was wondering if you would like to replicate the evening at Chepstow Community Hub & Library. I am sure it would prove popular with our customers!". I contacted them and a talk was initially arranged for April. Unfortunately, due to various circumstances, it didn't take place until October 2017.

Unfortunately, the wholesale sources of distribution that had been envisaged didn't materialise and Ben became interested in another project, totally different from publishing, so I suggested I took the remaining stock off his hands. By this time I was giving regular talks on Forgotten Gadgets so I felt that I would have no trouble in disposing of them through that avenue. This proved to be correct. Suffice to say I have only 6 copies left and they are not for sale, although I notice that now and again they appear on the internet for sale. I've just had a quick search now and I've found four second-hand copies with a starting price of £19.95 upwards, which is crazy when you consider that the new selling price was £9.95. Maybe they have become collectors' items already! Did you see that pig flying by?

Angel Hotel helps with book sponsorship

THE Angel Hotel is to help provide copies of the recently published "101 Forgotten Gadgets" to local Libraries

You may remember that some weeks ago we told you about Don Balkwill's forthcoming book, "101 Forgotten Gadgets" which was being published based on the "Grandma's Gadgets" articles that appear on a regular basis in the pages of this newspaper.

It can now be revealed that Abergavenny's premier hotel, The Angel, has sponsored thirty copies of the book to be distributed to the libraries in Monmouthshire, Torfaen, Blaenau Gwent and Newport.

The presentation of the books to the libraries will take place in Abergavenny Library on Friday, March 4 at 7pm.

"Knowing some of the financial pressures that libraries are under these days I approached William Griffiths, the General manager of the Angel Hotel, to ask whether they would be prepared to sponsor a number of books to be donated to local libraries, Mr Griffiths immediately agreed.", said Don.

"It something that I have done before, when my previous books about growing up on Dartmoor were published, a local clay working company sponsored a number of books to be donated to the Devon libraries".

After the presentation of the books, Abergavenny library they will be hosting a talk and quiz by Don where he will be showing a selection of gadgets previously featured in these columns, and asking the audience to try and guess (or remember) what they are.

All are welcome to attend so if you have any unusual objects that could be used in future articles or in the follow up book please bring them along.

Tickets are £3.50 which includes refreshments.

Meet Local Author Don Balkwill at Abergavenny Library as he takes us through

101 FORGOTTEN GADGETS VOL1

Do you know what this is?

Join us Friday 4th March 7.00 pm Tickets £3.50

On the left is a copy of a ticket. The 'teaser' object shown
is a Victorian egg topper in the shape of a Cockerel used for removing the tops of boiled eggs.

Can you think of anything misleading about that?

Cockerels don't lay eggs!

153

TRETIRE AND PENCOYD PCC
in partnership with
DAI LAUGHING PRODUCTIONS
presents

HISTORY IS MURDER!

A MURDER MYSTERY EVENING!

*A meeting has been called by the Knights of the
Keepers of the Wish to scrutinise an ancient
document puporting to be evidence of St Dyfrigs's
actual Wish... a Wish now worth a possible £7M.
Who would consider that worth murdering for?*

SO, THINK YOU CAN SOLVE THIS ONE?

MUCH BIRCH COMMUNITY HALL

SATURDAY 24th SEPTEMBER 2016 7pm for a prompt 7.30 start

Tickets £12.50 including 2 course meal and soft drinks
(bring your own alcoholic drinks if you wish)

Please book by Wednesday 21st September by contacting John & Margaret Oubridge
t: 01981 580233 e: oubridge@phonecoop.coop

IN AID OF TRETIRE & PENCOYD CHURCHES

History is Murder (Sept 2016)

My final Murder Mystery performance

By now Tom Ball had completely taken over the running of Dai Laughing Productions and was writing the scripts, organising the cast and arranging the rehearsals. Well done to Tom! This show was put on to raise funds for Tretire and Pencoed churches for whom we had performed before. Very few photographs were taken and none of Les Hayes, who was the murder victim and had 'died' at the beginning of the performance. (The first time Les had ever 'died' on stage?) I appeared purely as a cast member and it was absolutely wonderful. This was to be my last performance in a murder mystery. Do I miss it?. You may well ask, on the other hand, you may not ask, but I'm going to tell you anyway! I don't miss the work involved in organising things, but occasionally I have a yearning to put on just one more show. A big one to raise lots of money. Will it happen? I very much doubt it. Farewell Dai Laughing and good luck. (Sounds a bit melodramatic doesn't it? Well, that's just me)

L. to R. John Geraghty. Gill Crandon, Leila Gatrad, Tom Gibson,
Tom Ball, Janine Davies and me.

Always a good turnout for this organisation although the hall lacked atmosphere.

Forgotten Gadgets Talks

I mentioned that some of the suggestions and guesses given as to the use of an object were hilarious. One answer particularly sticks in my mind to this day. I was giving a talk to a pensioners club and one of the objects was the one shown below. It's like a pair of pliers but instead of jaws on the end it had a cone, when you press the handles together the cone opens up and spreads. It is called a 'Bec Du Canard', or in English, 'Ducks Beak' (I bought it in Corsica). When I asked the audience what they thought that these had been used for this little old lady, who must have been 80 years old if she was a day, said: "I know what it is, it's for young brides to take away on their honeymoon". The room erupted in laughter and I was left covered in confusion. There must be something about this weird tool because when I displayed it on the internet there was a lady from Ghana who confidently stated, "This tool was used during the slave trade era. Used in clipping the manhood of slaves that disobeyed their masters during the colonial era." Another lady suggested that it was "A barbaric tool for giving women smear tests". The imagination of some people amazes me.

Actually, these tools were used in the days when water was fed through lead pipes and this was used to spread the end of one pipe so another could be fitted into it, joining the two parts together. So, they are pipe expanding pliers.

Forgotten Gadgets Talks 2011 -2020

Within a few months of the Grandma's Gadgets articles appearing in the Abergavenny Chronicle in 2011 I started to receive calls from local organisations like the W.I., History groups, Probus, Pensioners clubs etc., all asking if I would go along to one of their meetings and give a talk on my gadgets. I was most happy to do so because as you have probably gathered I do enjoy standing up in front of a crowd and performing. I thoroughly enjoyed giving the talks and I'm pretty sure the audiences did too, because many organisations invited me back year after year.

Having had experience of public speaking I knew it was important, not only to engage an audience's attention but, to interact with them and if possible make them laugh. So I devised my talk so that the audience not only learnt about my gadgets but they could have the chance to touch them and guess what they were used for before learning what they actually did. This is how it worked. I would take along 20 unusual objects, each one being numbered, and laid out on a table. The audience would be split into teams, it didn't really matter how many people were in a team because it was just meant to be a fun competition, although, there were some who took it very seriously. I then ran through the objects one by one giving clues to their ages and origins. The audience were then given 10-15 minutes to come up to the table and have a closer look at the objects before writing down what they thought they were on an answer sheet provided. After returning to their seats I would ask each team what they thought the object had been used for before giving the answer, this is where the fun started because some of the answers were quite hilarious and imaginative (see facing page).

Year on year the number of bookings increased because I was asked to return to a lot of clubs and give another talk, obviously, with a different set of objects. Through recommendations I was also asked to give my talk to other organisations, which was very flattering. In 2018 I actually did 44 talks. Unfortunately, at the end of that year I was diagnosed with advanced-stage prostate cancer so had to cancel most of my bookings for 2019, because of the chemotherapy and radiotherapy treatment. The COVID-19 pandemic put paid to the 2020 bookings and I'm still in lock-down because I'm considered to be a person 'at risk'. For those of you with a ghoulish outlook the reasons for that are because I not only have cancer, I also have Diabetes, COPD, Lymphoedema, Spinal Stenosis, Sleep Apnoea and I'm prone to Cellulitis. How's that for a full house? Do you understand now why I didn't write a book about my illness?

Perhaps this really is the final curtain, or is it?

Just some of the Letters of Appreciation

"Everyone we've spoken to really enjoyed themselves which I'm sure you could tell from the response you received. A lot of people said they hadn't had such a good time in twenty five years!"

Enid Dyer, NSPCC Cymru Ponthir

"I write to extend my sincere thanks to you and your team for the superb entertainment provided last Saturday. It was obvious a great deal of thought and time had been put into both the writing and performance."

Cllr Martin Hickman, Mayor of Abergavenny

"I am so happy to confirm that Murder on the PCC was a huge success with the audience and the church who, thanks to Dai Laughing made a very healthy profit of £600.00 for St Teilo's funds."

Verley Toyah, for St Teilo's Mission Social Group

"Thank you so much for helping us raise such a marvellous sum for the NSPCC and for giving us such an entertaining evening. The feedback from all guests has been extremely positive. Everyone enjoyed themselves."

Ann Axford, Blaina & District NSPCC

"Ty Hafan extends sincere thanks to Dai Laughing Productions for the hard work and generosity raising the marvellous sum of £1030.00 being the proceeds from a murder mystery evening."

Gareth Luke, Director of Finance, Ty Hafan

"Just a note to say how enjoyable the evening of murder mystery was. We had problems convincing some members it would be a good night out, but it was, from the oldest to the youngest enjoyed it"

Gaynor Evans (Sec) Llantilio Crossenny W.I.

"We have received no end of phone calls this morning from guests last night saying how much they enjoyed the murder mystery and they want to do another one. You are a talented group of people."

Jenny Jones Sec. Llanarth Cricket Club

"CHADS charity performance at Abergavenny Borough Theatre. It was a superb performance and I have received some excellent feedback from friends and colleagues who really enjoyed the show."

Ann Walker, Hearing Concern

"I am writing to thank you for the excellent entertainment you gave us at our recent Fish and Chip Supper. It (The Watershed) was extremely well received and the acting and characterisation was excellent. As two of our care assistants said amid much laughter "so true to life"!"

Elaine Waddington, Crossroads Caring for Carers

"A really big thank you to yourself and the cast of Dai Laughing Productions for a really fun evening on Saturday and for supporting Help for Heroes, it is appreciated."

Diana McCrea, In support of Help for Heroes

"Thank you for your support and the donation of £500.00 from the recent Murder Mystery Dinner. It was a great way to raise both funds and get the community together and raising awareness.

Karen Murfet, RP Fighting Blindness

"Thank you for your brilliant performance, with your help we raised about £500.00 for Cancer Research UK Cymru.

Vernetta O'Connor, Barry and District Soroptimist's International

I would like to thank all those people who have appeared in any of the shows I have been involved with, you helped to make it enjoyable and fun. Many of the names are set out below but I know there may be others whose names I have forgotten so my apologies if I've missed you. (it's an age thing)

Alan Clouth
Alan Wilson
Andrea Hitchman
Anne-Marie Winslade
Angela Brinkworth
Anouska Lester
Bobby Waters
Bryan Green
Bryn Griffiths
Carmela Giafragna
Carolyn Gully
Chris Gray
Chris Smith
Christine Collingbourne
Christine Locke
Colin Adams
David Haswell
Dee Mahon
Della Middleton
Eddie Talbot
Elaine Evans
Emma Jane Morris
Emily Underwood
Fiona Angwin
Georgia Withey
Geraldine Rogers
Gill Crandon
Gwyn Jenkins
Harriet Geraghty
Helen Geraghty
Hilary Geraghty
Ian Phillips
Jackie Dafon
Jane Laurenti
Janet Richards
Jaycee Withey
Joan Paynes
Jodie Allinson
John Geraghty
John James
John Morris
John Owen
Jonathan Smith
Joy Newton
Kayleigh Malson
Kieth Davies
Kirsty Flynn

Kris Broome
Laura Collins
Les Hayes
Liz Gallagher
Liz Waters
Louisa Connelly
Louisa Jane Conte
Lynda Jones
Lynn Jones
Marilyn Balkwill
Marilyn Ritchie
Margaret Barrell
Mari-Anne Gibson
Martin Crandon
Martin Morris
Matt Beere
Matt Lane
Maureen Chadwick
Megan Guy
Mike Dennington
Mo Chadwick
Nick Watkins
Oliver Haswell
Pam Allinson
Pam Bush
Pam Pugh
Paul Dowell
Pauline Hughes
Raydene Blackmore
Rhona Hoffer
Richard Griffiths
Rob Gotobed
Rob Tollman
Ryan Howe
Samantha Christian
Sharon Lewis
Simon Griffiths
Sophie Murray
Stephen "Snowy" Clark
Sue Christian
Sue Phillips
Tom Ball
Tom Gibson
Tony Monaghan
Tony Tagg
Vikki Cartledge
Wendy Sinnot

159